THE EARLY SETTLERS OF COLRAIN, MASSACHUSETTS

—OR—

SOME ACCOUNT OF YE EARLY SETTLEMENT OF "BOSTON TOWNSHIP NO. 2, ALIAS COLRAIN," "ADJOYNING ON YE NORTH SID OF DEERFIELD."

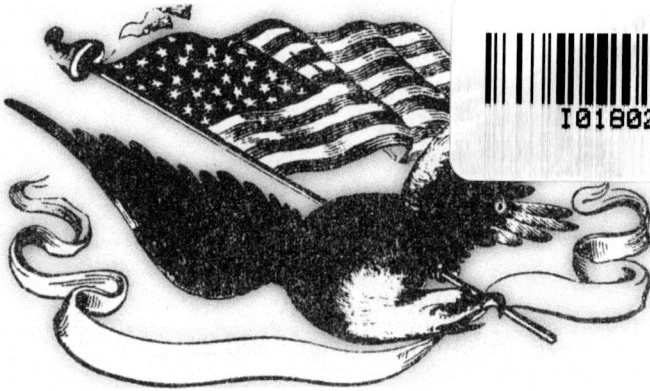

AN ADDRESS

Delivered before H. S. Greenleaf Post, No. 20, G. A. R., at Colrain, May 30, 1885

—BY—

Charles H. McClellan

HERITAGE BOOKS
2011

HERITAGE BOOKS

AN IMPRINT OF HERITAGE BOOKS, INC.

Books, CDs, and more—Worldwide

For our listing of thousands of titles see our website
at
www.HeritageBooks.com

A Facsimile Reprint
Published 2011 by
HERITAGE BOOKS, INC.
Publishing Division
100 Railroad Ave. #104
Westminster, Maryland 21157

Originally published:
W. S. Carson, Printer
Greenfield, Massachusetts
1885

International Standard Book Numbers
Paperbound: 978-0-917890-89-5
Clothbound: 978-0-7884-8619-7

TO THE PUBLIC.

It should be understood, that in putting forth the following brief pages, relating to the early times in my native town, I have not been impelled by any irresistable impulse to contest for literary honors.

Primarily, the purposes of their preparation arose from the belief, that as the older generation of inhabitants now living passed away, a knowledge of the facts relating to the times of their ancestors was becoming gradually obliterated; and from time to time I had collected much of the material, fact, anecdote, and legend, relating to those matters, trusting that those who should succeed me, especially my children, might at least to some extent profit by my efforts.

A very kind and flattering invitation from H. S. Greenleaf Post, No 20, G. A. R., that I should address them upon this subject, on Decoration Day of the present year, led to their preparation in the present form, and the repeated requests of my (I fear) too partial friends, have resulted in their reluctant publication.

Perhaps, however, it is not too much to hope, that a possible local interest may attach to them in the town to which they relate, and as the *descendants* of Colrain are very largely in excess of the present residents it is doubtless not impossible that they may attain to a still more extended circulation.

In what I have had to say, of the men of those times I have sought to

"nothing extenuate
Nor set down aught in malice."

But have desired that the *sons* should reverently recognize, what I esteem to have been the distingishing characteristics of their fathers, and that a just estimate be had of patient, unpretending, patriotic worth.

In point of time, I have touched upon most of the important matters relating to the history of the town, down to nearly the close of the last century. To accomplish this, the accumulated dust of nearly a century and a half had to be brushed away, a task requiring no little patient toil; and that some other, possessing greater attainments as well as more leisure, shall sooner or later appear to complete this effort, is the sincere wish of

THE AUTHOR.

Greenfield, Mass., September 1st, 1885.

ADDRESS.

Mr. Commander, Comrades of the Grand Army, Ladies and Gentlemen :— I trust I need offer you no apology for the subject of this address. The people and the times of which it treats certainly require no apology. And to me its seems enimently proper, that on this *Sabbath of Patriotism* when all over our broad land, a grateful people do homage to heroic deeds, and re-enshrine the memory of those, who though absent still speak from out the silence; that we should briefly review the story of that earlier generation of patriots, upon whose record we may well look back with pride. Early influences as well as my own inclination, have led me, ever, to greatly venerate the people who founded the institutions of this, my native town, and that up to the present time, no one of all their descendants, has in any adequate degree given utterance to the feeling of reverence and appreciation, of what they suffered and achieved, which is universally entertained, would seem to be in a measure inexplicable, and were it necessary, would constitute a proper vindication for what I have to say in their behalf.

I cannot claim that what I have to offer is history, and yet I indulge the hope that it may be an aid to some future historian of the town, whoever he may be and whenever he may appear.

It is the story of the wilderness and the log hut of the settler, and of young life commenced under far different circumstances than are ours to-day.

It is the story of earnest men and of brave, self reliant women, of hardship and privation, the cruel

savage and the dangerous beasts, the all surrounding
forests sheltered; in a word it is the story of

"Old trees, whose great and everchanging forms
Were shaped by nature in a hundred storms.
Old rocks, the red man's altar and his grave,
Old huts, the homes the early forest gave,
Old stories, gathered now from silent lips,
Old faces, lost in nature's last eclipse".

It will be a century and a half in a few days, since
the first events transpired looking to the settlement of
the good old town of Colrain.*   That its settlement
should have been so long delayed, to me seems somewhat remarkable. Deerfield, a neighboring and in fact
an adjoining town, was at this time quite an elderly
community, as also was Northfield, while Springfield
had been settled nearly a century. Capt. Turner's
fight with the Indians at Turners Falls had occurred
nearly sixty years before, and the sacking of Deerfield
long enough before to have been nearly forgotten,
had events in those early days crowded as closely
upon each other as they do in the times in which we
live.   I am aware that the "History of the Connecticut
Valley" says that the Smith Brothers, Andrew and
John, were in Colrain as early as 1732, remaining some
two years and returning again in 1736 to remain
permanently. Now I have serious doubts of their
being here as early as the first named date. That they
were here very early, and probably earliest of any of
the settlers, I have no doubt, but I hardly think they

*It will be noticed, that throughout these pages I have adhered to
the early mode of spelling the name of the town. Were excuse
necessary it would be, that up to, and long after the times of which
they treat, such was the early method, and the old residents. as I well
remember, greatly protested against the additional letter in each
syllable, as an unwarrantable innovation.

penetrated the wilderness of Boston township No. 2 previous to its being granted to the town of Boston.

From Aunt Roxy Smith, grand daughter of Andrew Smith, a very intelligent and well preserved lady of eighty, now residing in East Charlemont I get some account of the advent of the Smith Brothers. She says, that her grand father Andrew, and his brother, (but whether James or John she cannot tell, for he had these two and possibly three brothers, as there is a Robert Smith mentioned in connection in the early records) came to Colrain on horseback from Holden, Mass., with their axes in their saddle bags, and that on their arrival in the wilderness, just over the line from Deerfield, (for as you all know Shelburne was then a part of Deerfield) on the farm now owned by the Coombs Brothers, there was quite a strife between them which should strike the first blow in the new township. That they did not remain long but went back to Holden, returning soon after and buying land to settle permanently. This is in accordance with my own idea. They were two young, adventurous men, unmarried, and looking out for some new territory in order "to grow up with the country," and they came up into the wilderness on a prospecting tour having heard that a new township had been granted to the town of Boston, and was about to be opened up for settlement. But I do not think their visit was earlier than 1735-6, and am confident it was not six years previous to Andrew's buying his first land in town, which is the first recorded sale of land in the township, to a settler, January 10th, 1738.

But however that might have been, it matters little, the forest did not change much I fancy during the time they were first here, and there probably was not much of a market for the wood and timber they may have felled during the two or even six years they remained. The birch log in the spring which they are said to have placed is there today, and comparatively sound and permanent yet, as proof of at least a part of the story of their presence, but the first event of record looking to the settlement of the town occurred as I have intimated in June, 1735.

On Friday, June 27, 1735, "on petition of the Selectmen of the Town of Boston, by order of the inhabitants of said town, setting forth the great charges the said town is at for the support of their poor and their free schools and that they pay near a fifth part of the Province tax, and praying for a grant of three or four tracts for townships to be settled and brought forward as the circumstances of the said town of Boston shall require, or upon such conditions and limitations as this court shall judge meet." In the House of Representatives read and in answer to this petition:

Voted, "That there be and hereby is granted to the town of Boston, three tracts of land, each of the contents of six miles square and to be laid out in such suitable place or places in the unappropriated land of the Province for townships, by surveyor and chainman on oath, and to return plans thereof to this court for confirmation within twelve months. *Provided,* the town of Boston do within five years from the confirmation of the said plans, settle on each of the said towns, sixty families of his Majesty's good subjects, inhabitants of this province, in as regular and defensible a manner as the lands will admit of; each of said sixty families to build and finish a dwelling house on his home lot of the following *"dementions"* viz. eighteen feet square and seven feet stud at the least, that each

of the said settlers within said town bring to and fit
for improvement five acres of said home lot either by
plowing, or for mowing by stocking the same well
with English grass, and fence the same well in and
actually live on the spot; and also that they build and
finish a suitable and convenient house for the public
worship of God, and settle a learned Orthodox minister
in each of the said towns, and provide for their honorable and comfortable support, and also lay out three
house lots in each of the said towns, each of which to
draw a sixty-third of said town in all future divisions,
one to be for the first settled minister, one for the
ministry and one for the school. And in order that the
conditions of this grant may the more eventually be
"complyed" with, ordered that Elisha Cook, Esq., Mr.
Osenbridge Thatcher, Mr, Thomas Cushing Jr. and
Mr. Timothy Prout, with such as the honorable
board shall appoint, be a committe fully authorized
to admit settlers, and to take of each settler a bond of
twenty five pounds for the performance of the conditions so far as relate to their respective lots, which
bond shall be made payable to the Province treasurer;
and in case any of the lots in any of the townships
hereby granted shall not be settled in time and
manner as above provided, then such lot with the
rights belonging thereto, shall revert to be at the disposal of the Government."

In council read and "concurred and that John Jeffries,
Jacob Wendell and Samuel Wells, Esq., be joined in
the affair."

In pursuance of the above act, three townships were surveyed and are afterward known as

Boston townships No. 1, 2 and 3. No. 1 was Charlemont, No 2 Colrain and No 3 Pittsfield or Housatonuck as it was then called. A plan of Township No 2 was made by Nathaniel Kellogg, surveyor, and filed April 10, 1736, in accordance with the conditions of the grant and was approved by the Governor and Council June 15, following. The description is as follows : Beginning at a chestnut tree in Deerfield, north bounds, from which we run west 1777 perch to a stake and stones; north 2075 perch to stake and stones, thence east 1777 perch to stake and stones, thence south 2075 perch to the fore mentioned chestnut tree.

The terms of the grant, so far at least as they relate to township No. 2, were now complied with and the town of Boston was the owner and possesser of 23040 acres of forest in this frontier wilderness. It should be remembered here that this tract did not cover the entire township as it is now and did not include the Gore which was annexed in 1779. The east boundary of the old township commenced at Shelburne line on the Newell farm, now owned by Mr. Thomas Smead; running north it passed through Mr. Earl Shearer's house and just east of Mr. Joseph Bells,' striking Green river near Mr. E. D. Alexander's mill. It was the old story, and one hundred and fifty years have not changed the disposition of the town of Boston, in the least; she coveted a good big slice of the unappropriated lands of the province and set forth very plausible reasons for her greed, and as it has been ever since in the history of our state legislation she got about all she asked for.

As I said, she now owned the township, a pathless

forest tracked only by savages, and inhabited only
by bears and wolves; no foot of which I fancy any
inhabitant of the town of Boston had ever seen or
cared to see, nor had any other whitemen, except
the surveyor and chainmen, and possibly Andrew
Smith and his brother. The town of Boston so far
as I can discover, never took any steps toward
settling the town, they did not intend to, they had got
it, and proposed to realize upon it as soon as possible
Under date of July 14, 1737, I find a deed from John
Jeffries, John Armitage, Daniel Colson, Alexander
Forsyth, Caleb Lyman, Jonas Clark and Thomas
Hutchinson, Jr., Selectmen of the town of Boston, in
consideration of 1320 pounds in Province bills or as
we now reckon $6,600, one third in hand paid and
the rest secured, to be paid according to contract; to
Joseph Heath of Roxbury, 23040 acres the bounds
and discription being the same as those filed by the
surveyor the year previous, and also binding him to
the provisions contained in the grant, to the town of
Boston; and on the same date Joseph Heath deeds to
Joshua Winslow one third of his purchase and later
Gershom Keyes, (both these last gentlemen being
from Boston) acquires the other third, and both
coming in on the same basis as Heath had paid for
the whole tract. These men were now the proprietors
of the town, and seem to have taken immediate steps
toward its settlement, and I think showed very good
judgment in the plans they pursued toward that end.
They had evidently made a good bargain, and bought
the tract cheap, and as the sequel shows must
have made a large amount of money out of their
transactions. Their main object now was to attract

settlers to this new territory *and unload their wilder-ness*. To this end they caused to be surveyed out sixty lots in the south east part of the tract, of fifty acres each. They made the lots small I think for two reasons, first they wished to bring them within the reach of men of small means as most of the settlers doubtless were, and also to make the settlement as compact as possible, thus making it more easily defensible against the Indians. These lots were 50 rods north and south and 160 rods east and west, and lay in three ranges, reserving land for roads five rods wide between the ranges.

The first or east range, ran as far north as about where E. B. Stewart now lives, and the road between the first and second range ran just west of the Handy place, where Mr. Conant now lives, and on north past Mr. H. A. Howard's. The second range was laid out as far north as about a half mile north of Mr. Milo Miller's, and the road between the second and third range ran just east of the Coombs Brothers' farm, across the Stebbins pasture, so called, and just on the west border of Mr. Wm. B. McGee's farm, striking the present road where it is now travelled, by the Sprague place, and following it a short distance, but bearing west up on the hill side, it passed west of the row of maple trees belonging to Mr. G. W. Miller and came out just in front of his house, and so on north past the site of the old meeting house, striking North River at the bend which enclosed the island, near the Dennison place. The third range was laid out about 100 rods further north than where the meeting house stood, and the lots ran 160 rods west of the road I have just defined. These were the sixty lots that were anticipated by the terms of the grant and were numbered from one to sixty. Number one was the south lot in the first range, No. twenty-eight the south lot in the second range and No. forty-eight the south lot in the third range, although they are sometimes numbered differently in the discriptions in deeds, yet this is evidently the way in which they were numbered by the proprietors at the first. There were also a few lots laid out in the fourth range, and also other lots sold early that were not located in these ranges and whose boundary lines bare no relation to any subsequent divisions of land in the township; such as the Clark, Miller, Fairservice and Wells tracts. The Hugh Morrison tract is intended to be an extension of the third range, but is not regularly so, as the lines vary considerably. These 60 lots then, might be said to have been the basis for the settlement of the township, laid out to accommodate the needs of *actual settlers of limited means,* and in order to render it even more advantageous. I find that there is conveyed in the deed for each of these 50 acre lots (the consideration for which, is in most cases one hundred pounds, in current money of the province) the right to one hundred acres of undivided land in the north part of the town. It being, as the deeds rehearse, "one sixtieth of six thousand acres lying in equal "weadth" across the north part of the town" etc., so that the settler not only got his 50 acres, but the right to 100 acres more, which lots constituted what is known as second division lots, and which rights were held and sold by some of the settlers at least, even in advance of their actual settlement. The proprietors also bound the settlers in their deeds of the home lots, by the terms, substantially, of the original grant, and by which they were bound by the deed from the town of Boston. The early deeds, all or nearly all, containing the condition that they shall settle upon their lots, and otherwise fulfill the terms of the grant previous to October 9, 1740.

Such were the terms and inducements held out to settlers, and it would seem that they were not only wise but generous, and soon many adventurous and ambitious settlers from the older towns of Hampshire, and also Worcester and Middlesex counties, emigrated to the new township to partake in its opportunities and to enjoy what to them was not only a novel but a most grateful experience, *the actual possession, after years of struggle and privation in fee simple of the land they cultivated and the roof that sheltered them, and their wives and little ones,* Granted that it was a wilderness haunted by wild beasts and menaced by the savage Indians, but I tell you that Hugh Henry, Thomas McGee, Matthew Clark and John Pennill, felt themselves to be kings and lords of all creation, for was not the land on which they trod their own, and no landlord, as in the land from which they had come, could dispute their right to the possession and improvement of it. Yes, little, as the possession of land may seem to us in this day, it meant a great deal to those early settlers at that time.

SCOTCH-IRISH.

Colrain was settled, as you are aware, by Scotch-Irish, and perhaps a brief account of who and what these people were may not be uninteresting. They were mainly if not all of *pure Scotch parentage,* they or their immediate ancestors having emigrated from Scotland to the north of Ireland, on account of the inducements held out to them, to occupy and settle upon land that had been wrested from rebellious Catholic subjects. Their situation there was anything but pleasant, surrounded as they were by jealous neighbors, envious of their enjoyment of the land previously possessed by themselves, they took every occasion, even resorting to violence, to make their stay unhappy and to render desirable, emigration to some more congenial, if not so fertile a clime. They emigrated many of them from the Province of Ulster, from the towns about Londonderry and Colrain. They were and their descendants still are, "a peculiar people" of that blood of which it is said that "it will tell" wherever it is found.

They were intensely Protestant and generally Presbyterians and next to the devil they abominated a King. I have no doubt that some of them, or if not, their fathers and mothers, were present at the seige of Londonderry in 1688, the account of which is a sad tale of privation and suffering; indeed, there is mentioned in the history of that eventful seige, the doings of a youth named James Stewart and I have little doubt but that it was the same James Stewart who afterward settled in Colrain. In that terrible seige they defended the city until they had slain nine thousand of the beseiging army and until three thousand of their own number had fallen, and to such a state of starvation had they become reduced that a quarter of a dog was sold for five shillings and sixpence, horse-flesh was worth one shilling and sixpence a pound, a rat one shilling and a mouse sixpence; and it is related of an uncle of Hugh Morrison that having watched all day at a hole in the walls, in hope to capture a mouse that he might appease his hunger, the creature escaping into the wall at last, he burst into tears, realizing that his hopes of dining off that savory morsel had been defeated. Think you that after these experiences, a wilderness such as was this to which they came, infested by savages as it was, had any terrors for them?

They were brave, honest and God-fearing men,

"Stony and unapproachable in their pieties"

but possessed of a warmth and tenderness of heart, that you and I have felt and seen in their immediate descendants and which was strangly in contrast with their appearance and manner. They are said to have introduced the culture and spinning of flax, as well as the culture of the potatoe, into New England. They were frugal and economical and it is said that they were accustomed to walk barefoot to church; carrying their shoes and stockings in their hands, stopping when nearly there to put them on, and appearing at church fully dressed, and this has been told to me by their descendants whom I have known, now dead and gone. Borrowing and lending were very common among them, and buying and selling rare. If a pig or other creature was killed for home consumption, much of it was lent out to be repaid in kind in the future. All or nearly all of their subsistence, as well as the material for the clothing they wore was raised on their litttle farms, by their own care and toil; the delicacies and luxuries of life were not to be thought of, or if within their reach, the indulgence in them, would have been considered by those stern men and women from whom we sprang, hardly less then sinful, and from what I have come to know of them and their descendants, I am fully prepared to believe, that next to the disgrace of being publicly admonished by the tythingman, they estimated that of *"being out of pork."*

Superstitious they were, which is not strange in view of their surroundings; deeply religious, the Bible was their book of Books, and a thorough knowledge of the Westminster Assembly's shorter Catechism was imperative upon old and young alike.

Here they lived as brethren and neighbors, industrious and hard working people, quick to assist each other in trouble, and to care for each other in sickness and distress. And it is also a peculiar fact that the early settlers, who became permanent settlers of this town, very many of them were connected by the ties of blood relationship; they felt and cared for each other, and their descendants of the generations following were hardly less attached; and may God far remove the day, when that heartfelt attachment to our Kith and Kin, that remnant of old Scotch clannishness which we have inherited from our ancestors, and the inspiration of which we have drawn from our mothers, breasts, shall have ceased to exist amongst us.

Such as these were the people who began to subdue those forests, aud cultivate these. hillsides and valleys nearly one hundred and fifty years ago.

As I have said, the first recorded deed of land in this town, that I am able to discover, is of lot Number 50, or the third lot from the south end of the third range, to Andrew Smith, dated January 10, 1738. This is the first lot north of the Coombs Brothers' farm, on what is known as the Stebbins pasture.

During that winter quite a number of lots were deeded by the proprietors to settlers. James Smith bought lot No. 49, February 9, and John McCalester No. 48, probably about the same time, McCalester selling his lot to Smith the next year, and moving back I think to Pelham. James Brakenridge, and his son James Jr., from Kingstown, now Palmer, bought lots 51 and 52 during the year. John Pennell lots 57 and 58, settling I am confident where Mr. Aaron Lyons formerly lived, and where he built and kept the first public house in town, and which many years after he sold together with the east half of his two lots to John Wood. It was probably to this house that John Newman, the giant in courage but pigmy in size, brought the catamount he had killed with a club, of which the story is so often told. During this year Lieut. John Clark, Senior, of Worcester or Rutland, with several of his sons bought numerous lots; many of their deeds being dated February 9, 1738. John Jr., seems to have settled on lot No. 7, and his Brother Matthew on No. 8, both in first range. No. 7 being the lot where Mr. Copeland lives at present and No. 8 the next north. The home of the father, (John Senior,) during the time he resided here, seems to have been on lot 38, and which he willed at his death, about 1750, to his son Deacon George. Samuel, another son, seems to have settled on lot ¡No. 28, the south lot in second range, William on No. 32, Aaron Denio on No. 31, and James Clark bought lot No. 56 June 17, 1740, and I am confident settled upon it and he also, about this time acquired No. 55. James Barry was at this time owner of lot 59, and John Smith of No. 24, who about two years later, bought No. 33 and lived there. This lot in 1748 came into

with other old papers, some of which I should doubtless desired to have consulted, in the preparation of
this address. I have had some correspondence with
him, but he seemed loth to let the old warrant come
this way. It has however been published once or
more in the Gazette and Courier.

Its phraseology is so quaint and peculiar that
I give it here.

HAMPSHIRE S. S.

To Andrew Smith, one of the "prinsapel" inhabitants or settlers under
Joseph Heath of Roxbury, and Joshua Winslow, Esq., and Mr.
Gershom Keyes, both of Boston, the proprietors of No. 2 ad-
joyning on the north side of Deerfield : Greeting.

Whereas, application has been made to me the subscriber, one
of his Majesty's Justices of the peace, for the county of Hampshire,
by Andrew Smith, John Clark, James Barry, Alexander Harroun,
"Eliksander" Clark, John Pennel, Samuel Clark, Matthew Clark,
Hugh Henry, John Henderson, John Henry, James Clark,
William Clark, Thomas "Cockran," and Robert Hunter, all
proprietors in the above said land. 1st. To "chuse" a moderator.
2nd. Proprietors "Clark." 3rd. A Committee to manage affairs for
the settlement. 4th. To see if they will raise money for the times
past, and for the present year, and "chuse" a committee to provide
"preching" and all other officers as shall be thought to be needful.
6th. To consider all former acts and fit them to be put upon record.
7th. To see what they will do "consarning" a ministers' lot. 8th.
To have all former Treasurers and Collectors to bring in their
accounts. 9th. To see what "incouragement" they will give toward
building a grist mill, if any man will appear to do the same. 10th.
To see if they will buy a law book for the benefit of the settlers.
11th. To conclude on a method to call meetings for the "futer."
These are therefore in his majesty's name, to will and require you to
notify and warn the aforesaid proprietors, that they "assembel" themselves at the "Hous" of "Hew Heinry," upon Wednesday, the tenth
day of February next, at nine of the clock in the forenoon, then
and "thare" to act and transact in the affairs above mentioned.
This notification must be set up fourteen days before the meeting
and have you this warrant with your doings thereon. Hereof fail
not. Given under my hand and seal, this 27th day of January,

Anno Domini 1741-2 and in the 14th year of his majesty's King George the 2nd, Reign.

THOMAS WELLS.

This meeting was accordingly held, at the house of Hugh Henry, and where that stood I will endeavor to make appear before I close. Hugh Henry was elected moderator, Andrew Smith, Settlers' Clerk, Thomas Cochran, Hugh Henry, John Pennell, Alexander Harrmoun and Andrew Smith, Selectmen, or as they were called a "committee to manage the affairs of the town" and also other officers for various purposes. The records of this and the subsequent meetings of the settlers, show the sensible and straight forward methods of our ancestors in the transactions of public business. They were clear-headed old Scotchmen, knowing what they wanted to do and going directly to the doing of it. The advantages for education had been mainly denied them, and were we disposed to be critical, we might, to quote a slang-word, say that they were a little "off" in some of their spelling; but in view of the many phonetic attempts in that art, at this day, I am inclined to give them credit for being a century or more in advance of their age.

It seems to have required quite a number of meetings to get the young settlement fairly started in its career, and numerous meetings and adjournments were held during this and the following year, the record of which is exceedingly interesting to anyone who has a taste for matters so venerable.

FRENCH AND INDIAN WAR.

But we must leave the consideration of these old-time stories as shown in the records, at least for the present, for now there burst upon the infant settlement the dark and bloody struggle of the old French and Indian war, a struggle so cruel and long continuous, as to well nigh threaten to entirely wipe out this feeble frontier settlement. As I have said, the South Fort was probably built previous to this time, and perhaps Fort Lucas. The former stood on lot No. 51, on the east slope of what is called the Stebbins pasture, northwest of where Mr. Joel Cone now lives, and a few rods west of the line of the old south road; the site of it being perfectly apparent to-day. The latter stood where Mr. Henry A. Howard's barn now stands, on the lot that was afterward owned, but I doubt if it was at this time, by Andrew Lucas. They were doubtless log houses, probably two stories high with the upper story projecting, with port-holes arranged to command every direction, and here the settler with his long-barreled flint locked gun, and his wife with her kettles of hot water, that ever ready weapon of our grandmothers against Indians, and of their grand-daughters against tramps, gave their copper colored foe a very warm reception. These forts were built, I take it, by the adjacent settlers, for mutual protection. The name of Thomas Morris has always been connected with South Fort, and I am inclined to think that Fort Lucas is the same that is mentioned in the records as "Lieut. John Clark's fort," and that standing as it did near his home lot, (No. 38 where Charles Snow now lives) he might have been prominently engaged in its erection. On November 11, 1743, a grant of 100 pounds each, was made by the General Court, to Falltown, Colrain, and several other towns mentioned, for the purpose of fortifying the frontier, and a committee was appointed, "to lay out and erect in the most prudent manner, in each of the before named settlements, for their security during the war, a garrison or garrisons of stockades, or of square timbers, round some dwelling house or houses as will be most for the security and defence of the whole inhabitants of each place," etc. As a result of this, Fort Morrison was built, one of a cordon of forts, stretching across the northern frontier of the province, to prevent invasion from that direction. This fort undoubtedly stood where Mr. Samuel C. Avery's house now stands, well to the north end of what is know as the Morrison tract. It was larger, and more pretentions than the others, built with logs, but having a stockade, and I presume a mount or lookout from which the adjacent country might be reconnoitered for signs of savages. France declared war against England, March 15, 1744, and having granted a bounty on scalps to her savage allies, turned them loose upon the settlers; making their very existence, for nearly five years following, almost uninterruptedly, a source of direst terror and apprehension. Among the records in Boston, I find a muster roll of the men posted at Colrain, in 1747, under command of Lieut. Daniel Severance of Northfield, 43 in all, divided up between the three forts; and among them I find the names of John and Archibald Pennel, Andrew Lucas, Hugh, John and Robert Morrison, James Stewart, John Mills, John Henry, Robert Fulton, Alexander Herroun, Alexander Clark, Thomas McGee, John McCrellis and Thomas Morris. The following summer a Sergeant and 24 men, were stationed at Fort Morrison, and a sergeant and 15 men at South Fort, the names of the men being with hardly an exception the same as the year previous.

John Mills* of the garrison at South Fort was killed June 22nd, of this year as appears by the record. The treaty of Aix la Chapelle, October 7, 1748, was supposed to mark the close of the war, still matters were hardly tranquil for I find that from November 1st, of that year until the next April, Hugh Morrison, Andrew Lucas, John Pennel, James Stewart, Deacon Thomas McGee, Deacon Herroun, John McCrellis, John Henry and others, were still fighting Indians in Colrain, while Daniel Donelson was at Fort Shirley (in Heath,) and William Stevens was at Fort Pelham (in Rowe,) which argues that the wily savage was still abroad, crafty and murderous as ever, or else, which was possible in this case, these brave old fighters were following him from sheer force of habit. The peace of which we have spoken was of short duration. On account of difficulties at the west in 1754 or 55, the war with all its horrors, again broke out upon them. From August, 1754, to March, 1755, the towns of Colrain and Charlemont were garrisoned with 32 men under Captain Isreal Williams, with John Hawks as Lieutenant, and during the latter part of this year a garrison of 24 men was maintained here, and I find the record of another company under Isreal Williams, from October 18, 1756, to July 23, 1757, are "scouting westward," nearly the same names still appearing; also still another, from December 11, 1757, to April 14, 1758, bearing the names of John Hulburt, Joseph McKowen, John Cochran, John Henry, Abraham

---

*John Mills lived on lot 39 where Mr. Michael Johnson now lives. His widow Margaret afterward became the wife of Robert Fulton, who first settled on lot 36 and afterward owned much of the land on which the present village (city) now stands.

Peck, John Morrison, and other veterans showing that the settlers were still on the alert, and that "eternal vigilance" was the price of safety at that time. The two years succeeding, however, seemed to have bettered matters. January 21, 1758, it is ordered, that the garrison at Colrain "shall consist of 12 men and no more." The following year (1759) with the victory of General Wolfe at Quebec, and the surrender of Canada to the English, the war cloud lifted, and their savage enemies troubled the settlers no more. During this fearful time which we have described, many a brave settler lost his life, while defending his home and dear ones, and others including several women, mysteriously disappeared and were never seen or heard of again.

In May, 1746, Matthew Clark was killed by the Indians while endeavoring with his wife and daughter to reach Fort Lucas; the Indians pressing him hard, he endeavored to secrete himself under a log bridge over the run just west of where Uncle Thomas Brown now lives, and the Indians discovering him shot him. The wife and daughter, who seem to have been on horseback, reached the Fort, though not without being wounded, the latter with a bullet in her thigh, which she is said to have carried to her grave. This story is told in the "History of the Connecticut Valley" as being of the wife of Andrew Smith, which is correct in part. The young lady was Jane Clark, and afterward became the wife of Andrew Smith, and the mother of a large family. And it is a strange confirmation I find of this story, in the record of the settlement of the estate of this Matthew Clark, of which his widow, Jennet was appointed administratrix, December

11, 1746. Among the debts rendered against the estate are the bills of Dr. Hugh Bolton and Dr. Thomas Wells of Deerfield, "to attendance upon Widow Clark and daughter when wounded with the Indians", two pounds ten shillings, and four pounds and eleven shillings, respectively.

During this same year, (1746,) David, son of Captain Hugh Morrison, disappeared, and no tidings seem ever afterward to have been had of him. He was a young man, probably 25 to 28 years old or thereabout, he went out a short distance from the house or fort to shoot a hawk, the Indians surprised and captured him; it being impossible to pursue and overtake them in time to accomplish his rescue.

Near the old Indian Spring, 100 rods or more east of Mr. Benjamin Miller's, and the locality of which every school boy in the old south district knows, John Stewart (grandfather of Mr. Luther Stewart, whom you all know,) very neatly dispatched an Indian. Stewart had been hunting for a stray cow, and the Indian had found the cow, or if not, had found the bell which the cow had worn, and was occupying himself, in alternately ringing the bell and picking his flint, hoping, as it would appear, by the sound of the bell, to lure some unwary settler to his death. Stewart heard the bell, and his every sense being in those critical times fully alive to any signs of Indian deviltry, he imagined it did not ring just as it should, so taking to the bush he soon discovered the Indian and what he was up to, and killed him before he was aware.

In 1747, Mrs. Anderson, the wife of John Anderson

and great grandmother of Mrs. Luther Stewart, now living, was carried away by the Indians, at least her disappearance could only be accounted for in that way; she lived with her husband and family on lot No. 10, in the first range. She left the house one afternoon and went across the brook, east of the house, (the same as runs now, just west of Mr. Albert Nelson's house, and so on north,) to go to a cooper's shop and no trace of her was afterward discovered. Very many similar anecdotes I could relate going to show the terrible dangers which menaced the settlers, and the heart rending scenes and experiences which marked these years; but I will only give space to one other, and that relating to the exploits of John Henry, and John Morrison, a story which many of you have doubtless heard. Signs of Indians having been discovered near Fort Morrison, it was thought best to notify the settlers at the other forts; accordingly John Henry and John Morrison started out. The Indians pursued and fired upon them breaking Morrison's arm, but these intrepid men pressed on, and capturing a wild unbroken colt in the field, as they went, Henry held it, while he assisted Morrison to mount, and getting on himself, without a bit or bridle, he guided the colt across the river (probably at the old Nye ford,) and up over the hill to Fort Lucas.

The Indians are said to have known and recognized the men they were pursuing and avenged themselves by returning and burning Morrison's barn, and killing his cattle; the only instance of the kind that occurred during these times as I am aware; it seeming to be human lives and scalps the savages desired and not the destruction of property.

HIGHWAYS.

Let us now go back to the first town meeting, and consider briefly some of the matters which claimed the settlers' attention at this time, and among the first seems to have been the important one of Highways. As I have said, land had been reserved, in the surveying of the settlers' lots, for roads five rods wide between the ranges, and also for those of less width, at certain intervals, between the lots. But these as yet existed only on the surveyor's plan, and were not destined for many years yet to become what might be called dignified highways. The most that could be expected for the present, was the cutting down and removal of intervening trees for a safe passage on horseback, for as you know, the turnpike, and travel by carriage, were matters of the future, and the road scraper of our day was destined to come a little in advance of the telephone; the prediction of either of which would have fearfully startled those Scotch-Irishmen here in the woods, in 1742, and would have been valid ground for arresting the perpetrator of such a prediction, as being in league with witches. Still the means for inter-communication must be improved and accordingly three highway surveyors are elected; John Henry, of the North River road, John Clark, of the East Road, and William Clark, of the south road. The first of these is the same that is mentioned as being accepted by the town July 1st of this year, "the 'rod' that goes from the meeting house to the "furder sid" of John Henry's lot." This road must have been a terrible one to travel, as those of you who are familiar with the country between the old meeting house place and the old Nye ford are well aware; yet it was probably a much travelled road for twenty years or longer. The south road ran from the meeting house directly south, striking Deerfield line just east of the Coombs' Bros' farm. The east road, ran from the south road, east between lots 33 and 34 (or just at the north end of Mr. William B. McGee's farm) and over the hill past Mr Copeland's (or as it was then John Clark Jr.'s) to the east line of the town, where it connected with a road leading on down to Green River. This was undoubtedly the first road leading into town and was the one they travelled for many years in going to and from Deerfield. The town also, at this meeting accepted a road "from the west end of the third range to the 'Sammon hole'. This at once implies that salmon then came up North River and from the several references in the old records to it, I judge that the "Sammon hole," was not far from the locality of the present "City," and was probably the deep water a short distance north of the bridge. From the records, I judge that the north road was changed about 1759, to run further west through lot 59, intersecting with the road to the "Sammon Hole," which I imagine had been found easier to travel, and so striking the river about where the present bridge now stands, which road was long used and has been often travelled by many of the older genera-tion of inhabitants now residing here. The road be-tween lots 31 and 32 and which many of you have known by the name of the Handy lane, was laid out

very early, I think about 1743 or 44; and that to
Thomas Fox's March 3, 1765, and was probably the
first road laid out and accepted by the town, running
in that direction, and the agitation of the subject of
building a bridge over North River (a kindred subject and one the town has since had her fill of) was
commenced about 1766, though the bridge does
not seem to have been built until two years later.   I
will detain you no longer on this subject, than to add
an account of the building of a bridge across North
River in 1789, by one Henry Henderson as it appears
in the records.   A meeting was held April 6, 1789,
and a committee chosen to "treat" with Mr. Henderson regarding the building of the bridge. Their report
under date of May 11, of that year, embodies the
proposition of Henderson regarding the matter, and
is as follows: "To the Gentlemen, Selectmen of Colrain and other inhabitants concerned, would inform
you that Deacon Riddle and James McColluck hath
been talking with me respecting building a bridge
over the river known by the name of North River,
just below Abraham Avery's (probably near Elm
Grove) in said town, and I have agreed with the above
named men to build the frame of a bridge over said
river, and maintain said frame seven years from the
completing of said bridge, and that on special condition that the said Selectmen above mentioned, pay
me fifteen pounds lawful money's worth; one barrel
of New Rum by the 15th day of June next, as cheap
as it can be bought in Greenfield, by the barrel, and
the remainder of said fifteen pounds to be paid in
grain or suitable neat stock, at the completing of
said frame; and as I have a subscription paper which
will be void if said bridge is not planked and passable

by the first day of November; therefore must have the inhabitants of Colrain bound on their part to plank said bridge by the time above mentioned. This from your friend, HENRY HENDERSON."

Halifax, May 8, 1789.

The town voted to build the bridge, and chose Oren Smith, William Stewart, and Jonathan McGee, a committee to give and take bonds of Henderson. I have introduced this to show the bridge builders here of the present day, what the *motive power* was that built bridges 100 years ago, and that it would seem that the *New Rum* was a more important part of the remuneration than neat stock. I trust it staid in its place after it was built, at least during the term the contract required; though it would seem from the quantity of *"stimulant"* that Henderson was getting near, that it was in imminent danger of being floated down stream before the frame was even raised.

SCHOOLS.

The opportunities for gaining an education were very meager indeed, in those early times, and the accomplishments of the "three R's" were not by any means a universal possession, With cutting down forests, burning over and subduing the new country, clothing the bodies, and filling the mouths of the hungry little ones; for it needs not to be pointed out here, that our fathers and mothers of that day, for all the dangers which surrounded them, and the hard struggle to even exist which was necessary, they never failed to have a goodly quota of little ones about them. And how those little eighteen feet square log houses, held

the eight, ten, twelve, and even up to near a score, of
children of one family; and this not by any means an
exception either, seems almost a marvel to us in this
day. But such was the case, and with the additional
diversion (?) of fighting Indians; with an occasional
breaking up and going to the fort for a longer or
shorter stay; it is not strange that little attention was
paid to the matter of schools. It was not till March
5, 1753, that it was voted, "That the town will
have a school this year," and Hugh Morrison, John
McCrellis and others entered their protest against
having the school master or mistress paid by the lots,
but by the scholars that go to the school; implying I
think, at least in the case of Hugh Morrison, that he
had at this time more 50 acre lots, perhaps, than he
had children that were not grown up.

Previous to this, and during and after this time,
schools were kept at the houses of some of the
settlers; such a school was probably kept at the house
of Lieutenant James Stewart, who was one of the
earliest teachers, especially in the art of writing; and
who lived where Mr William B. McGee now lives;
a convenient center for the settlement about the south
fort. About 1770, three school districts, or squadrons
as they were called, were laid out, called the south
side, north side, and north river; and the school
houses were appointed to be built, one "near the
south west corner of James Stewart's lot," one "on
Robert Riddle's lot," and one "on the river above
*John Clark's," or just above where Martin Brown

*That no confusion may arise, regarding the persons of this name
I have mentioned, let me say that Lieut. John Clark (Senior) settled
where Charles Snow now lives, on lot No. 38 ; his son, John Jr., on

now lives. A school also was held at Lieutenant Hezekiah Smith's, and in one or two other places. I do not think, however, that these school houses were built previous to the Revolutionary War. A school house *was* built, probably about 1774 or 5, which stood as the records say, "at the bottom of the hill south of the meeting house,"or just at the east side of the present road as it reaches the top of the mountain, which was for some years, certainly I think till after the war of the Revolution was over, the only school house in town; which if it was the case, and I am confident it was, with the large township, six miles square, with settlers at this time scattered nearly all over it; those on the west side of north river and on Christian hill, must have had to take their schooling, as they were beginning to think they were taking their preaching, rather at arms length, still, they were undoubtedly accomodated with neighborhood schools nearer their homes. Here, in this first log school house, my grandfather, Michael McClellan, has told me, that he and his brothers and sisters went to school. Here he, and many of the boys and girls of that day, received all their mental training, to fit them for the positions of honor and trust which they afterward filled, and filled too with great credit. One thing those first schools did not lack, and that was scholars; indeed it has been told me that in the days not long after this, one hundred scholars was not an unusual number in the old south school house; where

---

lot No. 7, where Mr. Copeland lives ; and the one mentioned here was the oldest son of Matthew Clark, who was killed by the Indians in 1746 ; a grandson of Lieut. John, and father of Daniel Clark, whom many of those now living. remember.

there are to-day about five or six, all told. The appliances for training the youth have certainly improved, but the question in the near future, would seem to be, concerning the whereabout of the youth to be trained. After the close of the Revolutionary War, many school "Squadrons" were established, and school houses built, the records disclosing considerable trouble, in some districts in fixing the boundary lines; and a familiarity with the numbers of the various districts throughout the town will I think disclose to you their relative age and priority of establishment.

CHURCHES AND RELIGIOUS SOCIETIES.

As I have said, our fore-fathers were deeply religious men, staunch Presbyterians and strongly attached to the faith in which they were brought up; and on account of which many of them had in the time gone by, suffered persecution; thus around the old church and society, there clusters so much that is of interest, that a brief account of it would seem to be eminently proper and will I trust possess some interest to you.

By the terms of the first grant a meeting house must be built "for the public worship of God," and I have no doubt that the building was commenced the year the first settlers arrived, probably in the summer of 1738. It stood, as you doubtless know, on the top of one of the highest hills in town, just west of the old burying ground. The map indicates that it stood on lot 39, but this is evidently an error, as it stood, unmistakably, on lot 38. It was probably not nearly as large as the house on north river, which succeeded it, but was a frame building, the timbers being doubtless from twelve to sixteen inches square, readily procured from the "primeval" forests which surrounded it; (for I take it that "balloon frames" would have found little favor with the builders of that day, nor indeed were they adapted to the locality where this edifice stood;) with a shingled roof and entrance on the south side. It was innocent, I think, of window glass for years after, as it certainly was of a pulpit or pews, and from its advantageous location it did not need, nor have a steeple, nor, did the traditional bell, given by the grateful Irish lord, who was honored by the naming of the town, ever seem to have arrived.

It does not seem to have been but partially finished till after 1742, for at the second town meeting, held March 4th, of that year, Hugh Henry, Robert Hunter and Andrew Smith, were appointed a committee "to treat with the gentlemen," or proprietors about finishing it; and the town meeting held July 1st, of that year seems to have been the first meeting of the kind held in the new building, or as the records say, "the house in which they usually assemble on the Sabbath day."

The first committee to provide preaching consisted of John Clark, Robert Hunter and Andrew Smith, but just who was their first supply, (for they did not have a settled minister till about ten years later) is rather difficult to determine. Rev. Mr Abercrombie of Pelham seems to have preached for them, and boarded with Hugh Henry previous to July 1743. February 7, 1744, it was voted; "To continue the

Rev. Mr. Morrison sometime longer," and the September following it was voted "to have transient preaching, for the present continue amongst us, sometime longer according to our circumstances at present;" the circumstances probably being the impending Indian troubles.

In March, 1752, Hugh Morrison was chosen a committee "to represent our case to the Presbytery" and 200 pounds old tennor, 30 bushels of wheat, and 60 days work, were voted "to Mr Daniel Mitchel or or any other minister who will settle with us in the work of the ministree;" but Mr. Mitchel did not come. January 5, 1753, it was voted, "that the people have agreed to prosecute a call for Mr. Alexander McDowell;" March 5 they took some measures toward repairing the meeting house, and March 22 held a meeting; "to see which minister the town will choose whether Mr. Mitchel or Mr. McDowell;" and "voted and chose Mr. McDowell", also "to invite Mr. Abercrombie and Mr. Ashley of Deerfield" to come and keep a fast with us on the twelfth day of April next."

The historian of the Connecticut Valley wonders what this "Fast" means, which would seem to disclose that he was not brought up among the Scotch Presbyterians of New England. Considerable trouble seems to have been experienced in arranging the details for the settlement of Mr. McDowell, regarding the salary &c., and several meetings were held and committees appointed. The last of these held September 25, "at seven o'clock in the morning," seems to have settled it, and raises the question in my mind whether it was hardly fair to have called the meeting so early, as some possible objector might not have been an early riser. Alas! how the race have deteriorated, how very few of all the descendants of these good men would have had any sort of a use for a town meeting held at seven o'clock in the morning.

Mr. McDowell was settled as pastor of the church and society, September 27 of this year, and December 31st, Hugh Morrison is voted 42 pounds, old tennor, "for boarding ministers and two journeys on the towns business" and some "liqure" "spent at the ordenation." This to us sounds strange, but the customs of that time demanded it. Mr. McDowell's pastorate continued for about eight years, he being dismissed, it has been said, owing to his tendency to intemperance. He continued to reside here, died and was buried here, but no stone marks his grave; his family having neglected, and the town voting in 1768, not to procure any. As there was secured to him in 1761 the land to which the first settled minister was entitled, over two hundred and fifty acres in all, I cannot think that the town could properly be censured. After Mr. McDowell's dismission, Mr Abercrombie was again invited to preach to them, but some disatisfaction seems to have arisen and it was voted in August, 1763, "that ye Revd. Mr. Abercrombie should preach here no longer," and at the same meeting it was voted "to send to ye Jarses for Mr. Thompson" who seems to have been a "Touterer" in ye "Jarse" "College;" but nothing seems to have come of it, nor of several other efforts which followed. In In May 1764, Rer. Mr. Kincaid of New Hampshire was requested to "endeavor to write and bring a minister from Pennsylvania to preach with us and also to settle with us if we like each other," and I have in my possession an old letter of about this date a very remarkable and stately document written by the Revd. Mr. Abercrombie of Pelham to Lieutenant James Stewart referring to the matter I have just mentioned.

The meeting house seems to need repairing this year, and it is voted "to give any one the shingles on the south side who will take them off and return the nails to the town," and that Matthew Bolton "provide and frame in a "cell" (meaning doubtless sill) "in the south side" and also "to colour the meeting house" and ":that it shall be colored 'Blew.' " In 1766, an effort was made to have "Revd. Jonathan Levitt come and preach in town," and also the year following inducements held out to "Rev. Simeon Miller" to settle over them, but this last did not succeed. In January 1768, James Stewart was sent as a committee to Pennsylvania to endeavor to get Rev. Daniel McClellan "or some other Presbyterian minister;" though a vigorus protest was made at the expense of sending a man so far. After a great many preliminaries, as the records recite, Mr. McClellan came, though not till he had decided whether he should come or not by setting up a stick and letting it fall as it should happen; as it fell toward Colrain he came. John Bolton who sent for him, and accompanied him and his wife and their three colored servants here, being allowed nine pounds and thirteen shillings for his expenses. Mr. McClellan lived during the first year of his residence here on lot 37, in a house which then stood a short distance east of Mr. G. W. Miller's barn though after his dismission, he lived on the north part of what is now the Roberts farm, just south and adjoining the farm of Col. Hugh McClellan, His pastorate commenced June 1st, 1769, and continued about four years. During this time pews were built in the meeting house and it was voted "to pay for them by poll and estate assessed upon the inhabitants." In April, 1772, it was voted "to seat the lower part of the meeting house by real and personal estate and that it be done by last year's estimation, and to continue 3 years"; but when the committee, consisting of James Stewart, Dea. Hugh Riddle, John Clark, Dea. Harroun, Hugh McClellan, John Wood and Dea. Thomas Morris, had arranged it as they thought right, the town took it into their own hands, and voted "that the two highest persons in last year's estimation shall take pew No. 2, the two next highest the pew No. 3, and so on until the 38 pews are taken", but who by this arrangement occupied the pew of greatest dignity and who that of the least, will probably never be known. It had been voted in 1769, to build a pulpit, but it met with great opposition and resulted finally, though many years later, in the building of two meeting houses, one on North River, and one near where Mr. H. A. Howard now lives.

The project was carried along from 1769 to May 16, 1774, when an appropriation of twelve pounds was voted to build it and a sharp protest against the action of the town is entered upon the records, signed by John Morrison, David Wilson, Joseph Thompson, Daniel "Donetson" and others, living in the west part of the town. Nor can we wonder much at their action, when we consider what a hill they must climb to get to church, and that they should have protested against the permanent improvments which looked to the keeping of the Meeting House in a location that was convenient to the settlers as they at first settled, but not to the inhabitants of the town as a whole, is not in the least strange nor unreasonable. It is greatly to be regretted, however, that the building of a new pulpit should have so nearly rent the society in twain; but the trouble seems to have commenced here and to have increased as the years went on. In February 1777, Rev. Mr. Taggart was ordained and installed as pastor. In 1779 the building of a meeting house on the west side of the river was agitated, and a spot selected by vote of the town, "16 rods north west of David Morrisons house, in Capt. John Morrisons enclosure, at a stake and stones." This, would have been a move north-west with a vengeance, had it been carried out. The town, however, voted "to give the inhabitants on the west side of North River their proportion of preaching this year," but the meeting house was not built. It would take too long to relate to you, all the votes passed at the various meetings in the years immediately succeeding. In May 1780, it was voted, "not to build a meeting house this year at the place where the committee appointed;" and in July of the same year it was voted, "to choose a committee from out of town to look out a meeting house spot." Messrs. Jonathan Hastings of Charlemont, Benjamin Henry of Halifax, and Agrippa Wells of Greenfield, were agreed upon, and also voted, " that Mr. George Patterson and Capt. Hugh McClellan give their attendance on, and instruction to, said committee, with regard to the make of the town." This committee seems to have fixed upon a spot "near Mr Gardners, upon a rising ground northwest of his house, by a stake and stones set up for that purpose;" which location was accepted by the town; but just where it was would be difficult now to determine. Still it would seem that this knotty problem was no nearer

solution. In March 1783, and again in the same
month 1784, it was voted ·"that one third of the
preaching should be on the west side of North River,"
but in April of this latter year, the town voted, *"that
there shall be but one place for the public worship of
God in this town;"* which vote was substantially repeated in June 1785, and another committee chosen,
mainly from out of town, "to settle the controversy";
but not for sometime yet was it settled. It would
seem, too, that about this time, good old Parson
Taggart began to get disturbed, as I notice that in
Sept. 1785, James Stewart, Jonathan McGee and
Deacon Harroun, were chosen a committee "to con-
verse with the Rev. Mr. Taggart, with regard to the
request he laid before the Presbytery at their last
meeting, with regard to his dismission from his
pastorate;" and voted "to give said committee directions after they shall have conversed with Mr. Taggart what to write," which was, "that he be not
dismissed.''

In August 1787, it was voted, "to build a meeting
house near John Clark's where the committee appointed it, "as soon as conveniency will allow;" and in
May of the following year a committee was chosen to
procure materials; but yet in February 1789, this
committee were given orders to desist from their
efforts. And so the see-sawing in this notable controversy went on, and it was not till 1795, that a
larger and more commodious meeting house was
finally built, just north of John Clark's, who lived, as
I have said, where Martin Brown now lives. The
old church was taken down; and it is said that on the
day they met for that purpose, the two factions in this
meeting house controversy, had a pitched battle, and

that some of them were pretty roughly used; but
that it was all amicably settled before they separated
and no hard feeling was cherished afterward. And it
is also a probable fact that some of the timbers of the
old church building, were used by Capt. Clark
Chandler in building the house in which Mr. Geo.
W. Miller now lives. For me to attempt to describe
the new house would seem superfluous, as many of
you who listen to me have seen and worshiped in it.
Here, for nearly a quarter of a century afterward,
Parson Taggart instructed his people in the ways of
peace and Godliness, (the desk from which he spoke
being still used in your town hall to-day;) while they
watching their frosted breath as it icily ascended,
with every muscle tensely set to prevent the chatter-
ing of their teeth, devoutly sat and listened until he
had preached to seventeenthly and beyond in the
various heads of his sermon; the sun sometimes
getting behind the hills before he finished. For at this
time the heating of churches was a thing of the future,
and the right of it was seriously questioned. And it has
been told me, that when my good old grandmother,
Jane (Patterson) McClellan, by a little effort among
the women had procured a stove, it was talked
among the men that "they best get some trousers
for her," implying that her action was discountenanced.
Thus did our fathers seek to ostracise any warmth
in their churches, except such as pertained to the
doctrines preached.

Many good stories are told of Parson Taggart,
among the best of which is the account of his enjoyment of the hospitalities of good old Parson Emerson
of Conway. The occasion was a gathering of the
ministers of the county at that place, and Parson

Emerson had invited them to his house to be entertained. His wife having lived in the city previous to her marriage, was inclined to put on rather more style than some of her guests were accustomed to; the ample table cloth of snowy white damask, being quite a novelty to the assembled ministers, and quite in contrast with their furnishings at home. Parson Taggart was a large, rather corpulent, and very absent minded man, inclined to be somewhat careless in his personal appearance. As he sat at table, with the profusion of damask in his lap, the idea got possession of him, that a portion of his under raiment was escaping; and aware that he had on no suspenders, he modestly, but absent mindedly, from time to time proceeded to tuck it in. When the meal was finished and they all arose for the accustomed grace, there came a fearful crash among the good Domine's crockery; and Parson Taggart found that it was *not his shirt, but his hostess' snow white table cloth, that he had been tucking behind his capacious waist-band.*

Another, somewhat similar, relates to his having occasion to use a shoe maker's awl, and not being possessed of one he borrowed of his parishioner, Dea. McGee. When the time came to return it, arraying himself in his customary long black coat, he started out to do the errand, and make a friendly call upon the Deacon and his family. Arrived there, with his usual absent mindedness, the special purpose of his coming escaped him, and the hours sped by in pleasant conversation; nor did it occur to him till in shifting his enormous bulk in the chair he became vividly conscious of the presence of that awl in his coat tail pocket. This was "awl" that was needed; hastily rising, he handed it to the Deacon, remarking

"Mr. McGee here is your awl", and immediately departed for home. On one occasion, he started on horse back, to pay a visit to Rev. Dr. Packard in Shelburne. On the way, he had occasion to dismount to cut a stick for use as he rode; carefully trimming off the branches, he threw it away, carrying the open knife, which he had used, in his hand all the way to Shelburne. He was a very learned and thoroughly good man, greatly respected by all. Fourteen years he served as a member of the U. S. Congress, and is said to have read his Bible through once at least during each of the years of his service; a practice which perhaps not all the congress.men of the years succeeding have strictly adhered to. He continued to reside in town until his death in 1825, and among the best preserved monumental stones in the old burial ground are those of himself and family.

The same year that this house was built, witnessed the building of the old east meeting house, by parties in the east part of the town who were disgruntled at the location of this, and recently there came into my possession the records of this east society, from the time it started, on through its struggles and trials, until it finally voted to sell the meeting house and devote the proceeds to building the tomb in the cemetery near the brick school house. Before I leave this part of my subject, I wish (as being somewhat associated with it,) to refer to the old burial ground, and to several votes passed by the town which seem to go very far toward settling the question of its ownership.

By the old records I find that in March 1745, John Pennill, (Senior,) Robert Hunter, and Hugh Henry were chosen a committee "to take a deed of the grave yard on the part of the town" and in June following, it was "voted and granted one pound ten shillings, old tennor, to defray the charges of the grave yard deed." October 1767, it is voted "that the grave yard shall be fenced this year"; voted "that the west side of the grave yard shall be fenced with stones, and the rest with chestnut or oak rails." Also I find in March, 1786, "the bargain was confirmed by a town vote, concerning three-fourths of an acre of land adjoining the grave yard" which seems to have been purchased of Dea. George Clark.

Gentlemen, the present pitiful and disgraceful condition of this old burial ground, appeals to the sympathies of almost everyone present; here

"Each in his narrow cell forever laid,
The rude forefathers of the hamlet sleep,"

who while they lived, the sun did not shine upon *nobler, braver or grander* men. And that their last resting place should be thus desecrated, and the rude tablets which record their virtues destroyed, is a standing disgrace to the town, and to us as individuals. Could the order of the generations have been changed, and they have succeeded us, I am sure that our memories would not thus have been neglected.

SECOND DIVISION LOTS.

Let us again revert to a previous time in the history of these affairs. In April, 1743, the settlers voted "to have the second division land laid out as soon as possible", and also passed votes as to the size of the lots &c; but it was not for several years yet that it was done. Up to this time the six thousand acres which the proprietors had appropriated for this purpose, lying across the north part of the town had remained as at first. About 1751 or 2, the sixty,

one hundred acre lots were surveyed off and numbered, and the lots drawn for the settlers by Samuel
Clark, after which, notwithstanding the times were
"troublous" by reason of the Indians, the farms in the
north part of the town began to be taken up and
settled upon, though not to any great extent until the
close of the Indian War.

INCORPORATION.

In 1761 the town petitioned to be incorporated;
and chapter 10, of the old Province laws, recites; An
act for incorporating the Plantation called Colrain into
a town called Colrain.

Whereas, the new plantation of Colrain, lying in the county of
Hampshire is completely filled with inhabitants, and labors under
great difficulties and inconveniences, by means of their not being a
town : Therefore ; be it enacted, by the Governor, Couucil, and
House of Representatives :

Sec. 1. That the said new plantation commonly called Colrain,
lying on the northwest of Deerfield, in the county of Hampshire,
according to the bounds by which it was established by the General
Court, be, and hereby is, erected into a town, invested with all the
powers, privileges and immunities, that any of the towns of this
province do or may by law enjoy, that of sending a representative
to the General Court excepted.

Provided :—Sec. 2. That nothing in this act shall be understood
or so construed, as in any manner to supersede or make void any
order or orders of this Court now in force, respecting the methods of
making assessments within said plantation in time past, but that the
same shall remain, and be as effectual as if this act had not been made.

And be it further enacted :

Sec. 3. That Elijah Williams, Esq. be and hereby is empowered to
issue his warrant to some principal inhabitant of the said plantation,
requiring him in his Majesty's name, to warn and notify the said
inhabitants qualified to vote in town affairs, that they meet together
at such time and place, in said plantation as by said warrant shall be
appointed, to choose such officers as may be necessary to manage the

affairs of said town, and the inhabitants being so met, shall be and hereby are, empowered to choose such officers accordingly.

Passed June 30, 1761.

Signed and published July 11, 1761

The Indian disturbances now being ended, and the town incorporated; many of the settlers who had previously left their farms on account of the war returned, new accessions arrived, land was bought and settled upon in all directions, and a period of tranquility and prosperity set in, which soon put this young community well on the way to what forty years later it became, one of the most prosperous and enterprising towns in this part of Hampshire County.

REVOLUTIONARY WAR.

The period which will next claim our attention is the Revolutionary War; and it has occurred to me, whether or not, that provision in the act of incorporation depriving those Scotch-Irish ancestors of ours the choice of a representative, had any effect to increase their contempt for his majesty King George, and to strengthen their patriotic devotion to the cause of the Colonies. Undoubtedly it had; for no Irish "home ruler" of to-day, entertains such utter contempt for privileged rulers, as did they; and it is but natural to suppose that they were in hearty sympathy with the popular grievance of that time, "taxation without representation".

As early as September, 1768, I find it was voted, "that the town shall act on what the Selectmen of the town of Boston have sent to this town, and to send a man to Boston, to join the committee of convention there, that is now met, and that James Stewart, Jr., go as our committee man". It was about this time that

General Gage with British troops occupied Boston, and this recorded action probably bears some reference to that event, and proves that this distant frontier town was very early interested in the cause of resistance to the mother country.

William Stewart, James Stewart. Hezekiah Smith, John Woods, John Morrison, Daniel Donelson, and Thomas Bell, composed the committee of correspondence in 1773, and in January of 1774 a very significant town meeting was held. It seems to have been called to consider some communication from the committee of safety at Boston. Joseph Caldwell was chosen moderator, and then meeting adjourned to Mr. John Woods' tavern; (where Mr. Aaron Lyons formerly lived,) to discuss the situation, and other matters, including probably, certain liquids that John Woods naturally kept; and before they finally adjourned, they framed and passed some resolutions which are marvels of their kind, and fully justify the estimate I have put upon their authors. Undoubtedly James Stewart, and others whose names I have mentioned, had a hand in the framing and drafting of this remarkable work, and if the same abilities which they have here exhibited, still reside among their descendants, here or elsewhere, they certainly possess talents of a very high order.

These resolutions have been lost or abstracted from the records of the town, but I get them from another source, and deem it eminently proper that the record of this meeting should be given in their own words which are as follows. After receiving the letters sent by the committee of correspondence of Boston to the committee of correspondence of

Colrain and the proceedings of the town of Boston
also, the proceedings of a body of the good people of
the province were read; a motion was made
whether this town will conform to the firm resolutions
of our respectable brethren at Boston; the question,
being put, unanimously passed in the affirmative.

"Upon a serious consideration and due sense of our just rights,
liberties, and properties, look upon ourselves by the laws of natural
reason and common sense, to cast in our mite when our eyes behold
the daring insults of extravagant men, not only those the other side
the water, but men born and brought up as brethren with us, whose
famous abilities gave us just expectations that thay would die with us
rather than deny us, (but alas ! our hopes are gone ; designing men
had rather sacrifice their whole country, that was bought by their
and our glorious ancestry at the price of their blood, than give up so
small a profit), since they could not obtain their former desires as
they should get by a little detestable tea sent out by the East India
Company upon conditions unknown. We are sorry to see or hear
of any of Adam's posterity so blinded (if the light that is in men be
darkness, how great is that darkness). Now, in the present posture
of our political affairs, it plainly appears to us that it is the design of
this present ministry, to serve us as they have our brethren in
Ireland,—first, to raise a revenue from us sufficent to support a
standing army, as well as placemen aud pensioners, and then laugh
at our calamities, and glut themselves on our spoil ; many of us in
this town being eye-witnesses of those cruel and remorseless
enemies.

"From just apprehension of the horrors and terror of slavery, we
are induced to make the following resolves :

"First.—Resolved, That as freemen and Englishmen we have a
right to the disposal of our own, are certain there is no property
in that which another can of right take from us without our
consent, and that the measures of late pursued by the Ministry of
Great Britian, in their attempts to subject the colonies to taxation
by the authority of British Parliament. is unjust, arbitrary,
inconsistant and unconstitutional.

"Secondly.—Resolved, That by landing teas in America, impos-
ing a duty by an act of Parliament (as is said). made for the support

of government, etc., has a direct tendency to subvert our Consititution and to render our General Assembly useless and government arbitrary, as well as bondage and slavery which never was designed by Heaven or earth.

"Thirdly.—Resolved, That raising a revenue in America, to support placemen and pensioners, who, no doubt, when their scheme is once established, will be as merciless as those task-masters in Egypt, and will silence the murmurs of the people by laying on them greater burdens.

"Fourthly.—Resolved, That we do discountenance mobs, and unlawful and riotous assemblies; but when our valuable liberties and privileges are trodden under foot, and all petitions and remonstrances are rejected and treated with infamy and scorn, it is the duty of every true-hearted American (if possible) to free themselves from impending ruin.

"Fifthly.—Resolved, That the late proceedings of the town of Boston, assembled at Boston, to consult measures against the East India Company, have gained the approbation and applause of every true-hearted, honest man; and as their struggle is for the rights purchased by our renowned ancestors, which *we esteem as dear as life itself,* do fully express our satisfaction.

"Sixthly.—Resolved, That we will not, by ourselves, or any under us, directly or indirectly, purchase any tea, neither will we use any on any occasion, until that unrightous act be repealed, and will use our utmost endeavors with every person in our town as we have opportunity, that they shall do the same; and those that buy and sell teas contrary to our true intent and meaning, *shall be viewed as enemies to their Country, and shall be treated as such"*.

It needs not to be pointed out, that these are remarkable sentiments which our fathers have here left on record, regarding the momentous events which were then transpiring. Scarce less clearly is the true animus of the situation apprehended and set forth, by these plain men, in what they have here written, than it was two years later by the great patriot, Thomas Jefferson, in the immortal Declaration of our Independence. They plainly discover to us their opinions regarding the tax upon tea, and that the utmost resistance to the aggressions of the mother country was a first and paramount duty.

And too, I think there is expressed in these resolutions, which might well be called a prior Declaration of Independence: that which fully justifies what I have asserted regarding their, or their ancestors' experiences in Ireland, and the mighty influence they there received, tending to make them self-reliant, and rugged in their resistance to oppression from whatever source. They had felt in Ireland the crushing weight of this same hand of power and had emigrated to this forbidding rocky wilderness, to enjoy what they esteemed to be inherent rights, which were denied them there; and now the same oppressive influence, was proposing to attack them here, designing to absorb all the results of their hard-earned prosperty and to again reduce them to the position of dependant vassals. Happily, in this, the Mother Country was unsuccessful, and that, because our forefathers were just such men as they were and had encountered just the experience we have referred to. Following this, a committee was chosen "to post such persons as shall sell or consume that unnecessary article tea", and I have no doubt that the destruction of a shipload of it by dumping it into Boston harbor was to them a source of supreme satisfaction, as the resolutions very plainly intimate. John Woods, Hezekiah Smith, Hugh McClellan, Geo. Clark, Thomas Bell, James Stewart and David Harroun are the committee of correspondence in 1774, and about the same persons are a committee "to prevent mobs and riotous assemblies in town"; for it must be owned that not all were patriots, but that quite a number of tories were found here at that time.   But the patriots were so largely in the excess as to effectually over-awe them; and some of them, at least, were of such decided convictions upon these matters that an outspoken tory was liable to pretty rough treatment at their hands.   It is probable that the company of minute-men was organized and drilled during this year, in anticipation of the stirring events which it was fully believed could not be a great while longer postponed; so that when the news reached them that fighting had begun, the men of this town were ready to respond.

On the 19th of April, 1775, occured what is known as the Lexington Alarm, and "the shot was fired heard round the world".   The news was brought by men on horseback, alarming the towns as they came; one of them reaching Greenfield it is said, in the afternoon of the day on which the battle occurred, the news probably reaching this town before night.   The minute-men were hastily got together, to start at once for the scene of action.   How the 44 men that compos-ed this company could have been got together so quick-ly has seemed marvelous, living as they did, some in Shelburne, and scattered from there clear to the Halifax line.   But the time for action had arrived and like brave old Gen. Putman, "they stopped not on the order of their going".   It has always been said, that the company was quartered during this night before they left, at the houses of Capt. McClellan, Dea. McGee, and Dea. Harroun; camping down on the floor, what time they were not engaged in getting ready a stock of bullets for future use; while the wives and mothers are said to have spent the night frying doughnuts.   And I have no doubt such was substantially the case. I have often tried to imagine how they appeared as they started for Cambridge, on that memorable 20th of April; nothing very attractive in their looks, no great show of uniform; perhaps they had guns enough to go round and perhaps not, they did not always have, not till the battle commenced; but there were no hearts that quailed among them, and the experienced eyes that sighted those long gun barrels made it mighty dangerous to be within range of their muzzles. Their term of service at this time only continued about two weeks, though a large proportion of them re-enlisted. They were allowed nothing for entertainment, and at a town meeting held April 24, it was voted, "To send a waggon load of provisions to our men at Boston who have gone in the defence of their Country", and May 9th, following, voted; "to send nine pounds to the soldiers belonging to this town now at Cambridge"; and there is pathos in what follows, "that the selectmen do their utmost *to borrow said sum*". John Morrison and Dea. Wm. McCrellis are to meet at the house of James Stewart to prize some blankets that are to be sent, and May 23, Lieutenant Hezekiah Smith is chosen a delegate to the provincial Congress at Watertown.

I regret very much that there is a gap in the old records from Nov. of this year to March 1779, so that we lose any possible action of the town relative to the declaration of Independence, and the stirring events enacted during 1776. But we find that from February 23 to April 10, 1777, quite a number of Colrain men were with Capt. Lawrence Kemp of Shelburne doing duty at Ticonderoga, and in August of that year, a number of men connected with the minute-men, living in the north part of the town,

hearing the cannon at Bennington, hastily got together as many as they could of the company, and
post off on horseback as fast as possible, to help out
the brave Continentals under General Starke, but
arrive too late to do much fighting. In the two
months succeeding, however, this company is destined
to play an important part in the drama of events,
now speeding fast to a denoument. Burgoyne,
flushed with success thus far, was confident he
could carry all before him and by dividing the
colonies on the line of the Hudson River, thus fatally
weaken them; and so celebrate a happy Christ-
mas with Sir Henry Clinton, whom he expected to
meet at Albany. Our brave Scotch-Irish ancestors,
aware, as doubtless you are, of the fate of the lovely
Miss McCrea, and that a like fate was portended to
their own wives and firesides, should his success
be accomplished, needed no other incentive to resist
and crush this danger which threatened their borders.

In September, Col. David Wells, grandfather of
the present Col. David Wells of Shelburne, came from
the seat of war about Saratoga, to stir up the people
and induce them to rally for one last, resistless blow
upon their enemy, and whereas it seemed that every
man that could be spared had gone; the women,
imbued with the very spirit of Spartan Mothers, said
we will harvest the oats and care for the work that
is pressing, go and fight for your country. And
throughout this vicinity, from the Vermont line
as far south as Savoy, he took back with him 1500
additional men. So general was this rally that in a
time of wide-spread and deathly sickness which
followed, it is said that only the aged men and the
women were left to care for the sick and bury the

dead. Go not to ancient history for the record of deeds of surpassing heroism, but rather to the record of the deeds of those who filled our places, 100 years ago.

Forty six of the "minute-men" from this town, under Capt. Hugh McClellan went out at this time and were present at the surrender of Burgoyne in the following month; and the story of their exploits as told in "Holland's History of Western Massachusetts" is substantially correct, and Capt. McClellan was often wont to repeat it to his grand-children.

After the fall of Burgoyne, the theatre of war was removed to other and more distant fields, and while our fathers, never for a moment lost their interest in the cause, yet the record of the time is evidence of how hardly was our Independence achieved. The long protracted struggle was a fearful drain upon the limited resources of this young and over-taxed community, and as I read the record of the two succeeding years, it needs no stretch of the imagination to discover that these were times of dire extremity; the necessaries of life were fabulously dear, nothing was cheap except Continental money, the tories began to prick up their ears, plenty were ready to say "I told you so," and there begins to become apparent even almost among the tried and true ones, who were prominent in town affairs, a spirit of petulant murmuring and discontent, that a few years later broke out in open rebellion. In April, 1779, it was voted, "That no person belonging to any other town shall purchase cattle or any other provision in this town unless such person shall produce a certificate from the selectmen or committee of the town to which he belongs, that he is not a monopolizer or forestaller, and that he is a friend of the United States of America," and Oliver Newell, Lieut. Jonathan Wilson, and Deacon Harroun, were chosen inspectors of monopolizers and forestallers. Also I have under date of June 21, of this year, a communication from he committee of safety and correspondence of Boston, John Lowell Chairman; directed to the committee of this town; treating of this very matter, and showing that this evil was widely prevalent. And as discovering still more, their straitened circumstances, it was voted Sep. 20, 1779, to choose David Wilson, Oren Smith, James Stewart, William Stewart and Jonathan McGee, a committee "to state the price of hay &c.," and they reported that the price of hay be "thirty six shillings per hundred pounds, horse-keeping per night thirteen shillings, and oxen per night nineteen shillings." From some old letters in my possession, I also get some facts still further illuminating their perilous situation. The first is from David J effries, (a descendant of Joshua Winslow, one of the original proprietors of the town) under date of Oct. 15, 1780, written to James Stewart, the town clerk. Towards the close of his letter he says, "30 or 40 good tallow for candles and 40 or 50 good butter, would be very acceptable; candles and butter are at the high prices of 15 dollars per pound." The other is from Hartford, under date of Nov. 12, 1780, also written to James Stewart. Among other matters it says, "by the post you will receive three Spanish milled dollars, in hard money, equivalent to 240 Continental dollars par of exchange here". Thus we see that on a "hard money" basis, butter was worth about twenty cents per pound, or very near the average price it brings to day. But of gold and silver our fathers possessed very little, and that only of a foreign stamp, and were consequently subjected to the fluctuations of Continental paper money, and their situation was pitiful indeed. Thus too, do these old and venerable written papers, musty and yellowed by time, throw light upon the hard facts which existed away back in the time when liberty commenced in this land of ours, which now boasts sixty millions of freemen. I wish I might give you many other votes of a similar nature to those I have stated above, passed by the men of this town about these times; for I deem it they must possess great interest to us all; but am obliged to omit them. I must not however omit some account of a certain town meeting held in the year 1780, and which was one of the most extraordinary town meetings of which I have any knowledge, and, considering the size of the community, I do not think it has its parallel anywhere in the history of the state.

On the 13th of August, 1779, Hezekiah Smith was chosen "to go to Cambridge on the first day of September next, to help frame a constitution, or new form of Government, for the State of Massachuetts Bay". The convention met on the above date, and continued by adjournments till the second day of March following, at which time it adjourned until the first Wednesday of the ensuing June, and in the meantime the Constitution was submitted to the people for ratification. A meeting was held here on Tuesday, the 16th day of May, and Major Hezekiah Smith was chosen moderator. It was than voted "to read the Constitution paragraph by paragraph, or the clause, or clauses, and every person to make their objection, or objections, to any paragraph, or any clause, in said Constitution". This was accordingly done, and amendments proposed, discussed, and voted upon, to nearly every article it contained; after which, Major Smith, Capt. McClellan, William Stewart, Lieutenant Pennill, Oren Smith, Deacon Lucas, and Deacon McGee, were chosen a committee,"to draw up in proper order the amendments above, and also to make such amendments as they shall think proper on the remainder of the constitution", and to report at an adjourned meeting to be held on the 26th instant. This report under date of May 19, is very full and particular; stating their objections to various articles and giving their reasons therefor and is in every respect a most remarkable production. I wish I might introduce it here entire, but my space will not permit. They disapproved of the entire third article in the bill of rights, except the first seven lines, and the last clause of said article; and gave as a reason that they thought that the Legislature had "not a right to command the subject in matters of religion, unless in his protection." They disapproved of the qualification fixed for Senators (one hundred pounds) and gave as a reason, "we consider money as no qualification in this matter". They thought eleven Senators sufficient to constitute a quorum: "Reason,—to prevent unnecessary cost". They moved to amend the 2nd article of the 2nd chapter, regarding the qualification for Governor; "That the sum of one thousand pounds be not considered a qualification" and "that the word Protestant be substituted instead of Christian. Reasons,—1st., We could wish the important chair to be filled with qualifications preferable to that of money", and 2nd, "We are a Protestant people". In the 2nd Article of Chapter 6th; "We move that an addition be made to this article; that no person be suffered to hold any office in this Commonwealth who has not been friendly to the independence of said Commonwealth". Reason,—"A person who has acted the traitor in this important matter is not to be trusted".

These specimens must suffice; and I submit that in the light of events that have since transpired, the wisdom of many of their suggestions and criticisms, is fully apparent. A stranger, reading these pages in the old record book might well inquire, who were these wise philosophers, who discuss so ably the science of government? and the answer would be, they are the plain yeomanry of the land, the same men who have cut down these forests, and brought fertility to these valleys; unlearned, untutored men, their opportunties the slighest, for *the commonest kind of a common school education*; yet their wisdom, their candor, and their fearlessness, are so apparent in what they have here written, that the student who reads it after the lapse of a hundred years, cannot repress a feeling of pride that such men were our predecessors; and I predict that whoever may read it, when another century shall have closed; that in the light of the then current events, he will have no less cause for satisfaction.

Following these events, our fathers began to feel most sorely the force of their straitened circumstances. With the close of the war of the Revolution; serious embarrasments, both public and private, seemed to beset them at every hand. Nor were the reasons for this far to seek. Massachusetts had furnished one third

of the men to prosecute the war, and as her proportion
of the National debt she owed five millions of dollars.
On her own account she owed four millions more; and
to the soldiers she had sent into the field, she owed an
additional six hundred thousand; making her total in-
debtedness about ten millions of dollars; not much we
should say, in the light of our present liabilities; but
to our fathers, with revenues to meet this liability
only the slightest, with industries destroyed and para-
lyzed by war, with a people unsettled and debased by
the same cause, with taxes high, and a prospect that
they must be still higher, with stringent laws regarding
the collection of debts; which they conceived to be
and which doubtless were, unnecessarily cruel; *the
prospect to them was simply appalling.* And it is not
to be wondered at, that in view of all this; added to
the inflammable appeals and resolutions of designing
men; many of these brave veterans who had stood
firm where dangers were thickest, in the struggle
for independence; were swept from their loyal moor-
ings, and induced to take up arms against their couutry;
an act which to their dying day they regretted, and
remembered with shame and confusion.

SHAY'S REBELLION.

In the disturbances which followed, and which are
known as the "Shay's Rebellion", this town was
pretty thoroughly divided in sentiment, and the lines
very sharply drawn. Many recruits were furnished
to the ranks of the insurgents, while a still larger
number, I must believe, remained firm in their ad
herence to the cause of law and order. As early as

April, 1782, "the town unanimously voted, that it is the opinion of this town that the county courts ought not to sit in this county of Hampshire, in civil cases until the grievances they labor under are redressed", and "to send a petition to the judges of the supreme court at Northampton, and also a committee to go to neighboring towns to inform them of our proceeding"; and chose Geo. Patterson, Lieutenant Bell, and Lieutenant Riddle, as a committee. They then adjourned the meeting, for three days, at which time they met, heard the report of their committee and "voted that those who go to Northampton have ammunition out of the town stock"; and in the following month Geo. Patterson, Col. McClellan, James Stewart, David Wilson and Deacon Lucas are chosen a committee "to draw up the grievances we labor under, and lay them before the town for the town's acceptance and amendment; that they may be laid before the General Court's Committee provided they come to town".

It will be seen by this, that the attitude of the town was anything but passive, and this too nearly five years before these troubles resulted in any serious outbreak. A vote passed at the March meeting of 1783, disclosed somewhat, the circumstances they were in. Voted, "that grain shall be received for taxes at the following rates; wheat, 8 shillings, rye, 6 shillings, corn, 5 shillings and wool, 2 shillings and six pence, and that persons paying any of the above articles in lieu of money, shall deliver them at Major Smith's, Geo. Patterson's or James Stewart's." And as bearing upon their estimate of a "tory turn coat"; in May of this year they voted "that the people called refugees, that have gone to the British, shall not return to live amongst us." Rather uncharitable perhaps, but God bless them for their discriminating uncharitableness in this regard.

In August 1786, was held the famous Hatfield Convention and Colrain was probably represented by Lieutenant James Stewart. From this time on, matters ripened fast; the sitting of the courts was obstructed at Northampton and other places, and in January, 1787, occurred what is known as the battle at Springfield, the account of which is familiar to you all. Colrain was well represented on both sides that day, each doubtless believing they were right; but at the first shot the army of Shay's, which was really little else but a mob, ignominiously broke and fled.

They could not be rallied, and soon dispersed to their homes. When the men of this town arrived here they were dreadfully bitter regarding their townsmen who had remained loyal to the Goverment. Especially so were they regarding Col. McClellan and Major Wm. Stevens; these two they swore they would hang, but when their threats came to the ears of the Colonel's wife she merely remarked, "Haman built a gallows on which to hang Mordacai"; evidently having in mind an experience that Haman encountered in that little transaction. Their wrath soon subsided however, and March 21st following, sixty of them are recorded as taking the oath of allegiance administered by the Colonel; and with him also they were obliged to leave their guns; so that his bedroom, at the time is said to have presented the appearance of a small sized arsenal. Two days later appears the record of 25 more, subscribing to the oath before

Hugh Maxwell, Esq., of Heath. Certain restraints and disabilities, were imposed upon them for a short term, which they soon outlived, and the Shay's rebellion was a thing of the past. But not to be entirely forgotton, as the satirical prodding regarding it, which those who had remained loyal, always delighted to give their fellows; would hardly let the memory of it die. Two anecdotes regarding it have been preserved, and are perhaps worth relating. The first is of Deacon Riddle, and his son Samuel.

Deacon Riddle then lived where Mr. Gordon Thompson now lives at Elm Grove. His son Samuel, (father of the present Mr. Wm. Riddel of Greenfield), was a "Shayite" and went off with the others to Springfield. His father, the Deacon was loyal, and did not approve of his son's conduct; so hitching up his horses, he started after him. When he arrived at Springfield, the Shay's men were getting rather broken up, and some of them were deserting. He found his son, and told him to get into the sleigh and go home with him. Samuel obeyed, and they started; but before they had gone far, in passing a public house, they were halted as deserters; ordered to get out, their team unharnessed and put in the barn, and they were then placed in a room, containing but one small window, some distance above the ground, and the door securely locked. The Deacon, a pious, godly man; seeing a Bible lying on the table, opened it and commenced to read. He had not read long, when a a stranger came into the room, paused in front of the Deacon, and in no gentle manner snubbed the Deacon's nose. The covers of that Bible came together with the noise of a small earthquake; the Deacon rose in his wrath, seized the rascal by the back of the neck, and the most obvious portion of his pantaloons, and threw him through the window to the ground below, taking out glass, sash, and all. The Deacon then composedly returned to his Bible reading; the son Sam, during this time being a much frightened spectator of events, and neither of them knowing what next would happen. Very soon however, there is a rap at the door, and they are told that their team is ready for them to depart; it having been discovered, that the athletic Deacon was not the kind of a Shayite deserter they took him for.

The other story, is of Col. McClellan, and his neighbor Samuel Boyd. Boyd too was a Shayite, and at the close of the affair found himself in durance vile, with a strong probability that serious consequences lay not far ahead. His wife, sorely pressed with anxiety, besought the Colonel to intercede for her husband's pardon.

The Colonel with his characteristic kindheartness; and doubtless remembering the time when Boyd and himself had faced danger together, (for Boyd had belonged to the minute men) consented to go; so saddling "Old Pomp" he started for Boston. Arrived there, he presented himself before the Governor; (at that time no less a person than the redoubtable John Hancock, him of the severely classical and famous signature), interceded for Boyd and secured his release. After it was arranged, and while the papers were being made out, the Governor thought to give the Colonel a gentle reproof at being too kindhearted in matters of this sort. Said he;—"Col. McClellan, I believe if the devil himself should get into trouble, you would intercede, to have him set at liberty". The reply of the Colonel shows the quality of his wit, if not of his theology. "Certainly sir,—I should, if he repented".

FAMILIES.

I have spoken of the relationships which existed between very many families of the settlers, prior to their settlement in this town. Such was the case, and in the years succeeding, the marrying and intermarrying continued among them, until it might almost be truthfully said, that nearly all the inhabitants of the town were related to each other; constituting

> "So subtle a tangle of blood, indeed,
> No heraldry Harvey, could ever succeed
> In finding the circulation."

If I have not detained you to weariness, with this recital; and I somewhat fear I have, I would like to speak briefly, of some of the families that settled here very early, and the descendants of whom, some of them at least, have since remained uninterruptedly residents of this town. Prominent among these are the Clarks.

Lieutenant John Clark and seven of his sons, were among the earliest settlers here. His family were probably all born in the old country, and they doubtless came over from Ireland in the colony which arrived in 1718 or 19. They came to Colrain from Worcester or Rutland, (though John Jr. is mentioned as from Shrewsbury) having spent at least some part of the twenty years following their arrival in America, in those places.

They were here in Colrain in 1738, and during that, and the years immediately following, bought

largely of the settling lots;* and in 1745, the
father bought the 500 acre tract on the west
side of Norh River, disposing of a portion of it, very
soon after, to his son Mathew; from whom it descended, probably by inheritance to the fourth or possibly
fifth generation.

The Clarks were evidently people of means and
interested themselves largely in the welfare of
the new settlement, and were also active in its affairs;
John, (senior) having been Treasurer and Collector
from 1738 to September 1740.

The name of the wife of John Clark (senior,) was
Agnes Adams. The names of the children in the
order of their birth are as follows; Jane, who married
William Gray; Mathew, who married Jane Bothwell;
Thomas, who seems to have never married;
John, who married Catherine Montgomery; James,
who married Mary Clark; William, who married
Mary Smith; Samuel, who married Margaret Paul;

---

* It has been stated that the proprietors gave away many of the
house lots, to settlers, at first ; some authorities placing the number
so donated, as high as fifty lots ; and Joshua Winslow in a letter
written in 1751, to some of the settlers ; objecting to their proposed
petition to the General Court to have all the lands taxed ; claims
that forty home lots, together with the second division lots were so
disposed of. I have in my possession a copy of an old tax bill of a
few years later, in which all the land then owned by the proprietors
seems to be taxed ; which would indicate that neither the settlers or
the General Court, paid much attention to Mr. Winslow's demurrer.
Now while what is claimed above may be true, (and there is some
internal evidence going to establish it), yet from the knowledge I
have gained of the settlement of the estates of some of these early
settlers ; and that some of them at least, died in debt to these same
proprietors ; I am inclined to think that perhaps, Winslow was endeavoring to excite their sympathy, and that even at this early date,
this was an attempted case of tax dodging.

68

Elizabeth, who married John Stewart; and George, who married Alice, daughter of Deacon Alexander Harroun.

Of the sons, certainly six, and I think all, settled here. The one in doubt is Thomas; as I find no record of his owning land; but as he was unmarried, he undoubtedly lived with his father, on the homestead. The Clark geneology says that John Jr. settled in Pennsylvania; but that is, I think, a mistake: I am confident he settled in this town, and on the Copeland place, but did not live there many years, dying previous to July 11, 1742. The children of the two families, of the name who live here at present, (Joseph B. and John L.) are the seventh generation from Lieutenant John Clark, who have lived in town; and are descendants of Matthew Clark who was killed by the Indians in May 1746, as I have previously stated. And I am not aware that any descendant of any other branch of the family now resides here; certainly I think, none bearing the name.

Matthew Clark, oldest son of John, senior, with his wife, Jennet Bothwell (or Bothel, I get it both ways), settled on lot No. 8, as I have said, and were the parents of ten children, all but three of whom were born previous to their settling here. Of these Jane, married Andrew Smith; John, married Betsey Stewart; and is the ancestor of the numerous branches of the family hereabouts; Alexander, married Elizabeth Donica; and settled in Shelburne; Agnes, married Daniel Donelson; and has numerous descendants still living among you; William, married Mary Patterson; Elizabeth, married William Stewart; son of Charles Stewart; and her descendants are well known; Hannah married Joseph McKowan, (or McCowan), and was killed by the Indians, during the latter part of the Indian war; Margaret, married Peter Harwood, removed to Amherst, Mass., and afterward to Bennington Vt.; Sarah died, from drowning, unmarried; and Matthew, married Jane, daughter of John Workman.

As it may be of interest to some, certainly to those who are descended from him, I will allow space in which to introduce the will of John Clark, senior, a copy of which I have in my possession.

In the name of God, Amen. I John Clark, senior, of South Hadley, in the county of Hampshire, Province of Massachusetts Bay, Husbandman, being in perfect health of body, and in my right mind, but knowing the mortality of all mankind, am willing to settle my worldly affairs in the following manner. Imprimis; I give and bequeath to my beloved wife Agnes Clark, my whole household furniture, all my stock and chattels, and fifty acres of division land in a plantation called Colrain; she paying whatever debts may be found upon my whole estate.

Item. I give and bequeath to my son Geo. Clark, all my husbandry utensils, together with my home lot, buildings, and improvements, in the above named plantation, called Colrain.

Item. I give and bequeath to my daughter Elizabeth Clark, one note, of about ninety-four pounds from Elijah Alvord of South Hadley.

Item. I give and bequeath to my grandson, James Clark, son of my son John, deceased, one hundred acres of division land in said Colrain, with my gun and powder-horn; provided he stay with my wife until he be twenty one years of age; these things to be at her disposal.

Item. I give and bequeath to my daughter Jane Gray, fifty acres of division land in the plantation called Colrain.

Item. I appoint my beloved sons James and William Clark, executors of this my last will and testament. Witness my hand and seal, at Pelham July 15th, 1748.

R. ABERCROMBIE,
JOHN FERGUSON,   } WITNESSES.   JOHN CLARK, [L. S.]
A. ABERCROMBIE,

This will was presented for probate May 9, 1750, thus fixing quite closely the date of his decease. His wife does not seem to have long survived him; as November 13th, 1750, her son George is appointed administrator of her estate.

George Clark, or Deacon George Clark, as he was known, lived and died on the home-lot, where his son Noah, known to many of you, afterward lived; of whom it is told, that when the article of candle-snuffers, came into use, he was often known to praise the great convenience of the article, at the same time, snuffing the candle with his thumb and finger, and carefully depositing it in the cavity of the snuffers.

Andrew Smith, during his somewhat limited stay in town was prominent in its affairs. He was the first settlers clerk, and seems to have held many other positions of trust; but I find no mention of him in the records after March 22, 1745. He married Jane Clark, though not till after 1750, I think, and removed back to Holden, Mass., where he raised a family, died, and was buried. His son Andrew, married a Gragg, and lived in this town in 1788, afterward removed to Charlemont, where he reared a numerous family, and where his descendants now reside.

John Pennill (or Pannell), was another prominent man. He settled, as I have said, on lot 57. Most of his family were born previous to his coming here; only one son, Abraham, having been born in town, in 1742, the first white male child born in town. His son John Jr. seems to have inherited the homestead, or at least the east half of the two lots, 57 and 58, the west half going to Abraham. John Jr. was settlers' clerk from March 4, 1745, to March 4, 1754, and after the incorporation of the town, was town clerk from 1761 to 1764. He had a numerous family, two of his sons, John and James, marrying daughters of Hezekiah Smith. Beside John Jr. and Abraham, there were Archibald, Robert, and perhaps other children. Archibald married Esther, daughter of John McCrellis, and lived on lot 47; where he died in 1754, leaving four children, and his widow afterward married Deacon Andrew Lucas. Next to John Clark, it is probable that Hugh Morrison was the largest owner of land in town in those early times; and to him the settlers were greatly indebted for his public spirit and enterprise. He came here from Londonderry, New Hampshire, probably in 1739, having emigrated from the north of Ireland to that place about 1725 or 6. He and his brother-in-law, John Henry, in settling here, seemed to prefer going outside of the regular lots, and bought land up in the woods, on what was then the northern frontier of the town, and where the fort was soon after located. His wife was Martha, McCrellis; and their children were, David, Robert, John, Martha, Samuel, and perhaps others; the two last only having been born in this town. David was carried away by th Indians in 1746, as I have related. Of Robert I can give no further account John was a noted Indian fighter, and for a great many years a prominent man; he married, and raised a family of eight children, and it was through him the lineage descended in this town. He removed to Hartford, N. Y. where he died August 1st, 1810, aged 82 years. Martha, the first white child born in town, married Hugh, son of Dr. Hugh Bolton; and has descendants living at the west; and the only farther trace I get of Samuel, is in 1766, at which time he is living in Halifax, Vt. Hugh Morrison died, I think, not far from 1765, though the date of his death and place of his burial, cannot be determined, as no stone marks his grave. His wife died in 1772, aged 70 years; and a nameless grave, just to the north of her's, in the old burying ground, is no doubt, the last resting place of Capt. Hugh Morrison; one of Colrain's best and bravest veterans.

Thomas McGee, (weaver,) the progenitor of all of that name in this town, came here with his father-in-law James Stewart, from Concord, Mass. in March, 1742. He was at that time about 28 years old, and probably had but recently married his wife. He settled on lot 53; and for several years I think, his father-in-law lived with him. He was Deacon in the church for a great many years, a staunch, reliable man, thoroughly trusted in public and private affairs. He was above the average, I am sure, in educational attainments, as indicated by his signature which I have seen. He settled many estates and held town office much of his life. He died very suddenly, October 27th, 1793, aged 79 years, leaving a family of eight children; his son Jonathan succeeding to his estate, and to the public confidence which his father had enjoyed.

About 1748, James Stewart, (who is set down in the early records as a wig maker), seems to have separated from his son in law, Thomas McGee, and bought lot 32, and settled upon it; the house he lived in, standing in what is now Mr. Wm. B. McGee's pasture, near to the line of the old road, known as the "Handy lane". About 1754 he is joined by his son James Jr., to whom he deeded lot 33, which he seems to have acquired meantime. And from this time forward, for fifty years or thereabout, no man in town, was more a public servant than James Stewart Jr. He was settlers' clerk for several years following 1754, and was elected town clerk in 1764; and for nearly twenty five years following, with the exception of one year, the records of the town are kept by him. He was a beautiful penman, and it is a pleasure, at this time, to read what he has written, though much of it is more than a century old. He was a teacher of the art of writing, many coming from as far away as Greenfield to be taught by him. He served on many committees of the town, and was much employed in drawing of wills and matters of that kind. Respected and beloved by all, he filled a large space in the public estimation His first wife was Agnes (————) who died in 1784 leaving a numerous family. After her death, he married the widow Margaret Anderson. This lady, previous to her marriage to Anderson was the widow of John Kately, who lived on lot 54, and who died about 1752 or 3. She was the mother of the somewhat famous Hannah Kately, whose custom it was, to attend town meetings, and if affairs were not conducted as she thought proper, or seemed to encroach upon her rights; she was wont to protest against the action of the town, and have it placed on record; and some of the protests of Hannah Kately, the original "woman's righter" of Colrain, may be found in the old record book to-day.   James Stewart, Jr. died in 1809, at the ripe old age of four score.   His father James, senior, died in 1773, aged 93.

Ensign Hugh Henry, was another of the veterans of his time.   He came from Stowe, Mass., about 1740, settling on lot 34, and built his first log house a few rods southwest of where the south school house now stands, just at the east side of the line of the old road.   In this house the first town meeting was held, of which he was moderator, and for several years he was selectman and treasurer of the town.   His death occurred in 1746, leaving a wife and certainly five children, all young; the youngest being but four years of age.   He was great grandfather of Mr. Charles Henry of Greenfield, and of others of the name living in Heath.   In 1754, his heirs sold lots 34 and 35, to William Miller, and the last named lot has remained in the possession of Miller's descendants ever since.

John Henry (brother of Hugh) settled a short distance north of Samuel C. Avery's, on the farm afterward owned and occupied by James McCullock. His wife was Mary McCrellis, sister of Martha, the wife of Hugh Morrison.   He died about 1750, leaving five children. William, his oldest son removed about 1772 to Bennington, Vt. where some of his descendants, now live; others of them reside in Michigan; the wife of Governor Alger, at the present time Governor of that state, being a great grand-daughter of William Henry. James and John, next younger, removed to Cambridge, N. Y. and their descendants are numerous in that vicinity; and Andrew, the youngest son settled in Leyden.

The wife of John Henry was a remarkable woman, and had a most remarkable career. In her early life in Ireland, she married (—) Foster, by whom she had one child, a daughter, whom she named Margaret. Being left a widow she than married (—) Workman, by whom she had a son, John. Again left a widow, she emigrated with her two children to America, where she married Henry, by whom as I have said, she had five children. After his death she became the wife of Richard Ellis, who lived at one time on lot No. 10, and who afterward removed, I think to Ashfield. She outlived her fourth husband, spending her last days with her son Andrew Henry, in Leyden, and died there May 11, 1802, in the ninety-seventh year of her age. Her son John Workman, married Phoebe Stewart, sister of James Stewart, Jr., and settled on the farm where Mr. Ariel Hinsdale now lives.

Two families by the name of McCrellis, lived in town, back in the early times; John and William. The "McCrellis family records" say they were brothers, but I am confident they were not.

John McCrellis (older brother of Martha and Mary, mentioned above) settled on the Handy place and had a family of four children; dying May 3, 1759, aged 59. His oldest son, John Jr., married Hannah

McConkey of Pelham.   He fell overboard from a
boat and was drowned while shad fishing in Connecticut river in May, 1765, being only 25 years old,
leaving three young children; of whom Mary, the
youngest, married John Handy.   Another son, William, (or Deacon William as he was known,) lived at
one time, I think, on lot No. 1 of the third division.
He had numerous children, and his oldest daughter,
Jane, became the wife of Dr. Samuel Ross.

Esther, daughter of John McCrellis senior, married
Archibald Pennill, and afterward Andrew Lucas as I
have mentioned on a previous page.   Another
daughter, Margaret, married Ebenezer Wells, of
Greenfield. Of her children, John removed to Rowe;
Daniel settled in Greenfield, and was father of Judge
Daniel Wells, and grandfather of Colonel Geo. D.
Wells; the gallant Commander of the 34th Massachusetts Regiment, and who lost his life on one of the
battle fields of the Rebellion. Samuel, who also settled
in Greenfield on the homestead, and was father of
Ralph Wells, and grandfather of Mrs. Conant of
this town; who by a somewhat remarkable · coinci-
dence, now resides on the same farm where her great
great grandfather, John Mc Crellis first settled.

Let me here add a word regarding Hannah Mc-
Conkey, the wife of John McCrellis Jr.   After his
death she married in 1768, Archibald Thomas of
Rowe, and had nine children.   Of them, Elizabeth,
the eldest was grandmother of the wife of Major
S. H. Reed, afterward Sheriff of this County.
Mrs. Thomas, for years practiced medicine in Rowe,
and was probably the first woman physician in that
town. She died September 21st, 1825, aged 83 years.

William McCrellis, the progenitor of the other branch of the family in this town, was a nephew of John, senior. He came from the north of Ireland, and after arriving in this country stopped for some time at Noddles Island, near Boston. He probably came to Colrain in 1749, as under date of August 15, of that year he bought lots 48 and 49, the farm on which the Coombs Brothers now live. His first wife was Jane or Jannet McClure, who died March 13, 1763. His second wife was Jemima Mehany, by whom he had three children. Martha, who died unmarried; Elizabeth, who became the mother of William and Jonathan Coombs, also of Mrs. Flagg, Mrs. Hillman and Mrs. Dexter Wilson, now deceased; and William Jr. who had a family of ten children. William McCrellis died in this town November 3, 1781, aged 74.

Undoubtedly the first physician that ever practiced in this town was Dr. Hugh Bolton; who came here in 1741, buying lots 18 and 19 in first range, on one of which he settled. He was born and educated in England, where he studied medicine, and had built up a large practice. His decision to emigrate to America was somewhat suddenly taken, and the causes which induced his coming are quite interesting.

Dr. Bolton was a dissenter, and refused to pay tithes; an officer went to take his property, he resisted, a fight ensued and the officer was severly punished. In due time two constables were sent to arrest him; he saw them coming, and as they came in at one door, he, without waiting to even get his hat, went out at another. This was near evening. The officers, seeing him leave without a hat, did not

pursue him, believing that he would surely return.
But return he never did; he went to the nearest sea-
port, where he found a vessel ready to sail, on which
he took passage and in due time arrived safely in
America. This was in the year 1730, or thereabout.
He settled first in Londonderry, N. H. where
he bought land of Hugh Morrison in 1733.
He afterward lived in Peterboro, N. H. coming
to Colrain, as I have said, in 1741. He married Elizabeth Patterson:— her family afterward came to
America, settled in Baltimore, and one of the daughters
became the wife of Jerome Bonaparte. Mrs.
Bolton was drowned in Deerfield River, while
attempting to cross on the ice, January 30th, 1755. Dr.
Bolton died in this town June 8th, 1772, aged 85 years.
Their children were Hugh Bolton Jr., Matthew, John
and Nancy, also I think, one other son, Joseph, who
died young. Hugh Jr. married Martha Morrison, as I
have previously stated, and had six children. He
enlisted in his Majesty's military service, and was
killed in the French and Indian war. Matthew, the
second son, who was also a physician, married Hannah McClanathan of Pelham. She died December
28, 1761, and he married again but the name of
his second wife I am unable to state. He had five
children, all from the second marriage, three sons,
only, living to the age of maturity. Of these Mathew
Jr. married Electa Martindale of Greenfield, and settled in Heath; they had a family of, I think, nine children. Samuel, another son, married Jane, daughter
of Colonel Hugh McClellan, and settled in Rowe;
they had seven children, of whom Mrs. Mary Carley
of Jacksonville, Vt. and Jane, the wife of Alcanda
Preston of Halifax, Vt. are still living. Thomas, the

youngest, son of Matthew Bolton, married Fanny Cuthbert (I think) and settled in this town. They had six children. Matthew Bolton practiced medicine here, in connection with his father, until the time of his death; he outlived his father, only about two years, dying June 5, 1774, aged 43 years.

John Bolton, youngest son of Dr. Hugh, was a remarkable man, and his staunch patriotism should entitle his memory to be greatly venerated by the inhabitants of this town, many of whom are descended from him. His wife was Martha, daughter of Deacon Thomas McGee; by whom he had ten children. Of these, Elizabeth married Abraham Pennill, settled in Warren, Herkimer county, New York, and was the mother of Rebecca, wife of Captain John Wilson of this town. Rachael married Robert Lawson McClellan, son of Rev. Daniel McClellan, whom I have mentioned, and was the mother of six children; of whom, Jane married Rev. Jonathan McGee, and Caroline married Baxter Bardwell of this town, and still resides here.

Nancy, fifth child of John Bolton, married Robert, son of Robert and Margaret (McClellan) Miller. They had ten children, only two of whom, George Washington Miller of Colrain, and Joseph Warren Miller of Greenfield, Mass. are now living;* though her descendants of later generations are very numer-

---

*Hugh Bolton Miller of this family; descendant and namesake of Dr. Hugh Bolton; died in Colrain August 1, 1885. He was eminently qualified to have been the historian of the town; and among his papers will be found many valuable for historical, and geneological reference. I am indebted to him for the facts relating to the Bolton family, as well as other valuable information, all of which I desire at this time to gratefully acknowledge. C. H. M.

ous in this town and vicinity.   John Bolton was one of the most prominent military men of this town; he was in the last French and Indian war, belonging to the famous company known as the "Rodgers Rangers," and was in the battle of Quebec under General Wolfe, though at the time he was but about nineteen years old.   At the breaking out of the Revolutionary war, he with others raised a company of artificers, of which he was Lieutenant; John Wood being Captain. This company was in 1777 stationed at West Point. Captain Wood soon after received his discharge, and the command devolved upon Bolton, who was one of the bravest officers, as well as the best practical mechanic in this part of the colony.   He was chief engineer in the construction department at West Point, and was instrumental in putting the heavy chain across the Hudson river at that place, to prevent the passage of British vessels up the river.

About 1779, his men became discouraged; they were badly clothed and fed, had received no pay for a long period, and were almost in a state of mutiny. Bolton was engaged with his whole soul in the cause of his country.   He left the camp on a furlough, and came to Colrain, where he had a valuable property. He raised, by pledging his property, and otherwise, all the money he could; returned to West Point, and paid his men as far as it would go.   He, with his company remained at that place till the close of the war; they being Massachusetts men were discharged, but not paid, and were compelled "to work their way home" as best they could; enduring more from hunger and exposure, than they had for the same length of time, during the whole period of the war.

After a few years, Bolton gathered together the little fragments of his property, and emigrated to the state of New York, where he lived with some of his children. He was always inclined to look upon the bright side of things, until old age began to come on, which, with poverty, caused him to become pensive and somewhat moody, some years before his death; which occurred at Warren, Herkimer County, N. Y. in the year 1807, at the age of sixty-seven years.

Did time permit, I would speak of Deacon Thomas Morris, who settled where Mr. Joel Cone now lives, residing there until his death in 1781. Of Deacon Alexander Harroun, and his son, and grandson David; all men of note in their time. They came from Hatfield to this town, settling on what is now the Roberts farm, in the fourth range, in 1741, where the family resided till about the commencement of the present century, when they removed to Corfu, or Holland purchase, as it was then called, in western New York state, where many descendants of the family now reside. It was David Harroun, grandson of Deacon Alexander, who was at Springfield in the battle with the "Shayites". He was in Captain William Stevens' company of artillery, and when by accident the swab of one of the guns was blown away by a premature discharge; he thrust in his long brawny arm, and with his hand enclosed in a thick home-made yarn mitten, he swabbed out the gun.

William Miller, from Stowe, Mass., bought of Hugh Morrison, in August 1746, one hundred acres of land, "near where the east and west branches of North River unite"; now owned by Mr. A. A. Smith. The high water having made it necessary for him to remove his family from his house in a boat, during three successive seasons; he decided to seek a new location; and in 1754, he removed to higher land, buying out the heirs of Hugh Henry as I have previously stated. From him have descended the various families of Millers who have since been so prominently connected with the affairs of the town.

Hezekiah Smith, of Woodstock, Ct., bought of Joshua Wells, of Greenfield, what was known as the Wells tract, where his great great grandson Charles Smith, now lives; the deed being dated December 6th, 1764, and the consideration being 93 pounds, 6 shillings and 8 pence. He at once became prominent in town affairs, was delegate to the Provincial Congress and also to the Convention which framed the Constitution of this state; and represented the town in many other important matters. · His wife was Eunice Morris, daughter of Deacon Thomas Morris, and sister of Jane, the wife of Deacon Hugh Riddle, of whom I have spoken. His sons, Oren, Nathaniel, Hezekiah, Rominor, David and Calvin, all grew to manhood, and well sustained the prominence to which they succeeded, in public affairs.

Deacon James Wilson, (weaver) and his wife Margaret McGee, (sister of Deacon Thomas McGee), came to this town, from Chester N. H. He bought land, which his descendant Mr. S. N. Wilson now owns, of Samuel and Benjamin Munn, June 29, 1752. This farm was situated in Deerfield pasture; now Shelburne. Being a Presbyterian, and otherwise strongly attached to the church in this town; he bought, about three years later, of William McCrellis, three fourths of an acre of land in Colrain, for a house lot; and so became a resident of the town. Two of his sons, who at the time were quite well grown youths,

are said to have disappeared from the sugar camp
during the latter part of the Indian war, and were
supposed to have been captured; though what fate
befell them, whether they were killed or carried into
captivity; was never discovered, as I am aware. Of
his remaining sons; Jonathan the oldest, succeeded to
his father's estate in 1765; Robert settled where Mr.
Isaac T. Fisk now lives; Samuel where Robert Cone
now lives, both in Shelburne; and David, about this
time settled on Christian Hill, on land of the second
division. David Wilson was very active in town
affairs 100 years ago, and he is well remembered by
many of you, present here; for before me are many of
his descendants. His memory I have been taught
greatly to revere, as he was my great grandfather.
Sarah, the only daughter of his family that grew to
womanhood, became the wife of Colonel Hugh
McClellan, and so my great grandmother; so that as a
Wilson, I may be said to be "bred in and in."

As illustrating these matters, I will speak of but
one other, and that Jane Henry, sister of Hugh and
John Henry,—a brave, resolute, red haired woman,
who came from the north of Ireland, with her husband
Michael McClellan, about 1749. Her oldest daughter, Jeanette, had married Joseph Thompson in the
old country, and they probably came over in the same
ship as did her parents. In 1768, Joseph Thompson
settled on lot 56, in the second division, where his
descendant, Milo Thompson, now lives. Ann, another
daughter of Michael and Jane (Henry) McClellan,
married John Stewart, of whom I have spoken, and
and whose descendants are numerously represented
here. Still another daughter, Margaret, married
Robert, son of William Miller; from whom have de-

scended nearly all the Millers. Bear in mind that by inter-marriage, these lines have crossed each other many, many times since; and when I add, that David Wilson, Jonathan McGee and Nathaniel, David and Calvin Smith, married five of the daughters of Jeanette and Joseph Thompson; you will, upon reflection, begin to get some idea of this "tangle" in the lineage.

And thus; Comrades of the Grand Army, and friends; grateful for your kind and patient attention, and fully conscious that my words have done but ill justice to the theme; thus must I close the story of our predecessors in this community. Grand, noble, and true men, were they. Not great perhaps, as the world judges at present; but *great in courage, great in piety and faith, and great in all that is expressed by a noble manhood* In all these respects, they were giants in their time, and wrought as such. And during all time,—while the grass shall spring green from the low mounds beneath which they sleep; the story of their achievements shall be delightful to peruse. The work which your patriotic endeavor accomplished, was but the complement of what they had performed. With hands few and weak in comparison, they struggled heroically, to conquer an eternal independence for this land of ours, and thus humbled the pride of the proudest nation the sun had, or has ever shined upon. Yours was the opportunity, to establish by your valor, the truth; that here, in this land which their devotion had founded,—liberty shall live eternal. Among your noble fraternity,—of the sons who were worthy of their sires; let the memory of their heroism never be forgotten. Cherish their names, their deeds, their virtues; nor doubt that in the far vista of the years,—the grateful generations shall inscribe like

honor to your deeds; and that which they have suffered, and that which you have achieved, shall be,
alike, held in everlasting remembrance.

ERRATA.

Page 10, line 2, for Housatonuck. read Pontoosuc.
" 13, " 11, for bare. read bear.
" 22, " 8, for Harrmoun, read Harroun.
" 24, " 12. for pretentions. read pretentious.
" 25, lines 22 and 25, for Isreal, read Israel.
" 38, line 29, In. — is superfluous.
" 39, " 19, for vigorus. read vigorous.
" 40, " 31. for improvments, read improvements.
" 53, " 28, for this, read the.
" 55, " 8, for denoument, read denouement.
" 64, " 11. for Gordon, read Gurdon.
" 67, lines 4 and 15. for Mathew, read Matthew.
" 78, line 27, for Mathew, read Matthew.
" 79 " 16, for Rachael, read Rachel.

In behalf of the numerous other errors, of typography as well as punctuation ; I bespeak a charitable criticism.

INDEX

This index covers all names in the text, including the family skeches. Women are indexed under both married and maiden names where known.

DENIO, Aaron 18
DENNISON, 12
DONELSON, Agnes 68 Daniel 25
  49 68
DONETSON Daniel 40
DONICA, Elizabeth 68
ELLIS, Richard 75
EMERSON, Parson 43 44
FAIRSEERVICE, 13
FERGUSON, John 70
FISK, Isaac T 83
FLAGG, Mrs 77
FORSYTH, Alexander 11
FOSTER, Margaret 75
FOX, Thomas 31
FULTON, Robert 24
GAGE, General 49
GARDNERS, Mr 41
GEORGE (king of England) 48
GEORGE II (king of England)
  22
GRAGG, 70
GRAY, Jane 67 70 William 67
HANDY, 12 75 John 76 Mary 76
HARRMOUN, Alexander 22
HARROUN, Alexander 21 68 81
  Alice 68 David 52 81 Dea
  40 42 53 57
HARWOOD, Margaret 69 Peter
  69
HASTINGS, Jonathan 41
HAWKS, John 25
HEATH, Joseph 11 21
HEINRY, Hew 21
HENDERSON, Henry 31 32 John
  21
HENRY, Andrew 75 Benjamin 41
  Charles 74 Hugh 14 19 21
  22 36 45 74 82 83 James 75
  Jane 83 John 21 24 25 28-
  30 71 74 75 83 John Sr 19
  Mary 74 William 74 75
HERROUN, Alexander 19 24
  Deacon 25
HILLMAN, Mrs 77
HINSDALE, Ariel 75
HOWARD, H A 12 40 Henry A 23
HULBURT, John 25
HUNTER, Robert 21 36 45

HUTCHINSON, Thomas Jr 11
JEFFERSON, Thomas 49
JEFFRIES, David 57 John 9 11
KATELY, Hannah 73 74 John 73
  Margaret 73
KELLOGG, Nathaniel 10
KEMP, Lawrence 54
KEYES, Gershom 11 21
KINCAID, Rer Mr 38
LEVITT, Jonathan 39
LOWELL, John 57
LUCAS, Andrew 23-25 71 76
  Dea 59 62 Esther 71 76
LYMAN, Caleb 11
LYONS, Aaron 18 49
McCALESTER, John 18
McCLANATHAN, Hannah 78
McCLELLAN, Ann 83 Ansel 19
  Capt 53 59 62 Caroline 79
  Col 63 65 Daniel 39 79
  Hugh 39-41 52 56 78 83
  Jane 43 78 79 83 Jeanette
  83 Margaret 79 83 Michael
  34 83 Rachael 79 Robert
  Lawson 79
McCLURE, Jane 77 Jannet 77
McCOLLUCK, James 31
McCONKEY, Hannah 75 76
McCOWAN, Hannah 68 Joseph 68
McCREA, Miss 55
McCRELLIS, Elizabeth 77
  Esther 71 76 Hannah 75
  Jane 76 77 Jannet 77
  Jemima 77 John 24 25 33 71
  75 76 John Jr 75 76 John
  Sr 76 77 Margaret 76
  Martha 71 74 75 77 Mary
  74-76 William 75-77 82
  William Jr 77 Wm 54
McCULLOCK, James 74
McDOWELL, Alexander 37 Mr 38
McGEE, Agnes 73 Clarence 19
  Dea 44 53 59 Jane 79
  Jonathan 19 32 42 57 72 79
  84 Margaret 73 82 Martha
  79 Mr 45 Thomas 14 19 24
  25 72 73 79 82 William B
  19 30 33 Wm B 12 73
McKOWAN, Hannah 68 Joseph 68

WILSON, David 40 57 62 83 84
James 82 John 79 Jonathan
57 83 Margaret 82 Mrs
Dexter 77 Rebecca 79
Robert 83 S N 82 Samuel 83

WINSLOW, Joshua 11 21 57
WOLFE, Gen 26 80
WOOD, John 18 40 80
WOODS, John 49 52
WORKMAN, Jane 69 John 69 75
Phoebe 75